"Practical 'how-to' guides can make pastoral ministry more effective and more fruitful. This is especially true in the average parish which has to rely on many volunteer ministers. Samples of forms and letters are great time-savers, especially for new ministers.

"In *The Parish Activities Handbook*, Owen Meredith draws on his own vast experience to offer a large selection of options for organizing an effective parish ministry. Chapter 2 alone, Administration and Stewardship, is worth the price of the book. Filled with many time-savers and practical organizational wisdom, this handbook is a must read for anyone involved in today's parish ministry. I hope all training programs for the parish ministry make Meredith's *Handbook* a required text."

William J. Rademacher, Ph.D.
Author, *Lay Ministry*
and *New Practical Guide for Parish Councils*

"Owen Meredith's *The Parish Activities Handbook* is, as its subtitle proclaims, a very practical guide. Methodical and detailed, it gives a disciplined and rational approach to programs and processes that will make a parish work. In most parishes, dominated by the feeling-sensate people, this handbook offers common-sense advice on how to get things done."

Rev. William J. Bausch
Author, *The Total Parish Manual*

"*The Parish Activities Handbook* deserves a place in every rectory because it reinforces a simple truth: parish activities require sound planning. A well-planned activity shows respect for parishioners, and this book's many forms, checklists, and sample letters make planning easy.

"Planning also expresses a commitment to justice. The *Handbook* offers guides to the job descriptions of parish employees, advice on the solicitation of funds, and methods for including everyone in parish communications. These heighten parish consciousness of the need to do to others as we would have them do to us.

"Refining your program of parish formation? Developing new ministries? Enhancing parish hospitality? Fostering liturgical participation? The *Handbook* offers tried-and-true ideas; it guides parishioners from setting initial goals to evaluating finished projects. It is indeed a book for every parish staff member."

Dr. Mark F. Fischer
Pastoral Council Columnist, *Today's Parish*
St. John's Seminary, Theology Department
Camarillo, CA

"Owen Meredith's *The Parish Activities Handbook* proposes both a system for parish organization and oversight and a series of possible steps or actions in connection with each of the proposed areas of ministry. As Meredith says, his book may contain even more than you will ever need to know.

"He considers the Pastoral Council and eight areas of ministry which he wants to see the Council keep on its agenda: administration and stewardship, communication, education and formation, family life, parish life, social action, worship and spiritual life, and the missions.

"Meredith does not talk in generalities. When he talks about the Parish Pastoral Council, for example, he tells what it is in two sentences and then moves immediately to five rules for successful meetings. Many of us who are stumbling around looking for practical guidelines and advice on how to get things done in any area of parish life and ministry will appreciate this parish cookbook.

"The author has many recipes for better parish administration and stewardship as well as specific proposals for "parish family nights" and "fellowship coffees," for spiritual growth activities, and for religious education programs. He covers the field and does it well. *The Parish Activities Handbook* is going to be a welcome addition to the 'how to' shelf of any parish leader."

Rev. Jack Gilbert
P astor and *Today's Parish* Columnist

PARISH ACTIVITIES HANDBOOK

A Practical Guide for Pastors, Staff, Councils, Committees, and Volunteers

OWEN MEREDITH

TWENTY-THIRD PUBLICATIONS
Mystic, CT 06355

Twenty-Third Publications
185 Willow Street
P.O. Box 180
Mystic, CT 06355
(860) 536-2611
800-321-0411

ISBN 0-89622-671-9
Library of Congress Catalog Card Number 95-78540
Printed in the U.S.A.

Dedicated to

My Wife,
Mary Virginia,
with Love and Gratitude

Acknowledgments

In many ways this book is a compilation of ideas and programs which I have put together for presentation as a unit. Many persons gave their time and skills to help, and I am grateful to each of them. Some of the contributors are listed below.

The Cathedral of the Incarnation, Nashville, Tennessee:

Rev. William J. Fleming, Rev. Patrick J. Kibby; Staff Members Darleen Reilly, Annette Peek, Lori Reddick, Dicky Wilson; Parish Pastoral Council Members Marie C. Boyd, Esther Cook, Kristy Dixon, Leonard and Virginia Maginn, Greta Menke, Joseph Pelletier, Penny Powers, Anne Greene Rolman, Wayne Suite

The Diocese of Nashville, Tennessee:

Teri Hasenour Gordon, St. Philip Church, Franklin; Harry Hosey, Director, Adopt-A-Parish Program, Old Hickory; Bob Kimball, Fiscal Services, Nashville Diocese; Ann K. Krenson, Vice-Chancellor, Archives and Records, Nashville Diocese; Rev. Stephen A. Klasek, Diocesan Planning and pastor of Holy Rosary Church, Nashville, TN; Boo Martin, Immaculate Conception Church, Clarksville, TN; Sister Adrian Mulloy, R.S.M., Director, Ministry Formation Services, Nashville Diocese; Theresa Patterson, Director, Haiti Parish Twinning Program, Nashville; Anthony J. Spence, Editor, *The Tennessee Register*; Ramona Stejskal, Secretary to the Bishop of Nashville; James F. Walsh, Jr., Deacon, St. Matthews Church, Nashville

Also:

Nancy Brown, Bonita Springs, FL; Ed Fox, President, Fox Insurance, Fairview, TN; Cathy Gustavson, St. Joseph Church, Libertyville, IL; Jean Knight, American Red Cross, Nashville; Sue Lyons, Church of St. Stephen, Des Plaines, IL; Jerry Meade, Tom Mathis Music, Sarasota, FL; Lois Meadows, Executive Secretary, Nashville Area Chapter, American Red Cross, Retired; Dennis I. Mudd, St. Joseph Church, Libertyville, IL; Martha Recher, Director, Tennessee Valley Blood Services, American Red Cross, Retired; Miss Virginia Wright and Walter Wright, Saints Peter and Paul Church, Winter Park, FL

Contents

Introduction

The largest church in the world today is the basilica of St. Peter in Rome, which has space for 60,000 if everybody stands. One of the smallest is Les Vaubelets church in the Channel Islands, which has room for one priest and a congregation of two. I am pleased to report that both churches can profit from this book.

The church nears the year 2000 with fewer and fewer priests and women religious to handle the work of its expanding parishes. A strong parish pastoral council is important. So are active parish groups and committees. Suggestions in this book are designed to support and assist your pastor. Clear with him and work with him in all things.

The size of your parish does not matter. Organization does. Workers are necessary, of course, but each worker should have a well defined assignment and proper guidelines. On the pages of this book you will find parish tasks outlined in an orderly fashion with topics ranging from annual budgets to zinnias for the altar. Do you know how to tackle a church inventory? See Chapter 2. Do you need a mail permit? See Chapter 3. Have you decided to institute a children's liturgy of the word? Chapter 8 tells you how. Do you need to raise money for a new building? An entire section in Chapter 2 is devoted to fund-raising.

Devote time to defining work assignments. Center in on assignments that will best get the job done in your parish. See that committees set deadlines, and meet them. Schedule meetings on a regular basis. Always take time to discuss programs, recognize progress, provide inspiration and guidance.

This guide was organized with eight parish committees in mind but you might want to adapt. I have outlined the thrust of each committee, made membership suggestions, and defined goals and objectives. You will find certain topics expanded in a final section entitled, "Specific Projects in Detail."

This book will cover more than you, your parish, or your council will ever need. So simplify, eliminate, and consolidate.

The vineyards are waiting. The fields are ripe. It is time to go forth.

Chapter 1

The Parish Pastoral Council

What is a parish pastoral council? What does it do? The council provides an avenue through which laypersons can participate in the life and action of the church. Every parish needs a strong pastoral council.

Meetings should be scheduled each month. They should be dynamic and carefully structured.

Five Rules for Successful Meetings

1. Keep them prayerful. Never forget that the council is made up of lay volunteers seeking to carry out the mission of the Lord. Begin and end each meeting with a prayer for guidance, dedication, and inspiration.

2. Start on time. Only a few members may be in place at the beginning of the first meeting, but persevere, and the second meeting should see everyone on hand at the appointed time.

3. Follow an agenda. A suggested agenda:

A. Call to order

B. Opening prayer

C. Roll call

D. Read and approve minutes of previous meeting

E. Reports from committees

F. Old business

G. New business

H. Closing prayer

I. Adjournment

Council members should receive copies of the agenda for each meeting.

4. Seek consensus but remember Robert's Rules of Order. Meetings often fall apart because members interrupt reports or speak out of turn. The council chairperson should propose that members refrain from addressing the assembly without obtaining the floor, and should not claim the floor a second time if there are others who wish to speak the first time. Also,

---

PARISH PASTORAL COUNCIL PRAYER

*Lord,
Help us be on hand for all who seek you.
Guide us each day in our actions,
service, celebration, and prayers.*

*Be with us in the service
of our parish,
and in the work you would have us do.*

---

they should not speak on a motion while the vote is being taken. Consensus is sought after adequate time has been devoted to discussion.

5. *Close on time.* In parliamentary language, a motion to adjourn "takes the place of all other questions whatever," and with good reason.

Presenting Reports

A. Review programs that have been completed.

B. Present outlines of programs that currently are in progress or are planned.

C. Define any problems that have been encountered.

D. Describe assistance that is needed.

For example, the communications committee chairperson might report that the next issue of the parish newsletter has been completed and is being distributed, that a monthly calendar of activities is being prepared, and that publicity is under way for an upcoming craft fair, but that information for the calendar is slow in coming, and help is needed in distributing craft fair posters. The chairperson might then ask for suggestions about speeding the collection of facts and figures for the calendar, and about who might help distribute the posters.

What Is Consensus?

People reach consensus through prayerful discernment, discussion, respect, and trust, according to a handbook by Ministry Formation Services, Diocese of Nashville. Consensus is a general agreement by members of a group on an opinion, position, or proposal. The essence of consensus is intellectual agreement: coming to a common understanding of a position and agreeing to the validity of that position.

The majority vote approach produces winners and losers, as the MFS handbook points out. Individuals opposed to a position before the vote may still be opposed after the vote. Less than full support can be expected from a group in such a situation.

In consensus, however, general agreement is sought. The formula:

A. Treat others with respect.
Listen to what every person has to say without prejudging his or her positions. Show respect for these persons and consideration for what they have to say.

B. Take time for necessary discussion.
(1) Free and open exchange continues until each individual's position has been heard and understood.
(2) At this point the chair might summarize what is perceived as the points of agreement and disagreement.

C. Search for general agreement.
(1) Attempt to whittle down areas of disagreement.
(2) Ask individuals to reclarify these points and discuss them.

D. Formulate a conclusion.
(1) Mutual agreement can be reached with acknowledgment of the validity and acceptance of another's position.
(2) If consensus does not occur and sufficient time has been given for discussion, there may be a need for further research and prayer. Drop the matter and move on with the meeting. Deal with it later when the group has had time for reflection.

PARISH PASTORAL COUNCIL BYLAWS

First Act of your Pastoral Council: Formulate a Set of Bylaws

The best place to start is with your diocesan guidelines for pastoral councils. There are a variety of models being used by councils today. What follows here is one such model, which has been adapted from an Advisory Council Plan written by James F. Walsh, Jr., Deacon, Nashville Diocese. It is used with his permission.

PREAMBLE

We, the members of the (name of parish) (city and state), in order to be more expressive of our faith, do hereby declare ourselves willing to become active in the mission of Our Lord, Jesus Christ, by sharing with our pastor the burden and responsibilities of our parish community, in accordance with the Decree on the Apostolate of the Laity, Vatican II, the Canon Law of the Roman Catholic Church, and the statutes for parishes of the (name of diocese).

ARTICLE I—TITLE

Section 1. This organization shall be known as the (name of parish) pastoral council.

Section 2. The council shall constitute the Parish Board of Directors.

ARTICLE II—PURPOSE OF THE COUNCIL

This council shall collaborate with the pastor in making major administrative decisions affecting the parish and shall assist the pastor in accomplishing his mission.

ARTICLE III—STRUCTURE OF THE COUNCIL

Section 1. The council shall function within this framework:

A. Chairperson
B. Vice Chairperson
C. Recording Secretary
D. Treasurer
E. Youth Representative
F. Eight Committees:
   (1) Administration and Stewardship
   (2) Communications
   (3) Education and Formation
   (4) Family Life
   (5) Parish Life and Evangelism
   (6) Social Action
   (7) Worship and Spiritual Life
   (8) Missions

Each committee shall include a chairperson, vice chairperson, and committee members.

The pastor and associate pastor shall be "ex officio" members of the council.

Section 2. Any matter of council concern shall fall within the jurisdiction of one of the committees. The council chairperson shall determine the committee jurisdiction of any particular matter. Should a dispute arise, a majority vote of a quorum of the council shall govern.

Section 3. The council chairperson and vice chairperson shall jointly resolve all incidental matters referred to the council by the pastor or committee chairperson for settlement where time does not permit consideration by a quorum of the council.

Section 4. A quorum of the council is defined as any called meeting at which a majority of voting members is present.

ARTICLE IV—COUNCIL MEMBERSHIP

Eligibility—Anyone who is enrolled on the

records of (name of parish) and who is 18 years of age or older shall be eligible for council membership by election or as otherwise provided below. (Exception: Youth Representative)

Section 1. Voting members of the council shall consist of the following:

Elected Members:
A. council chairperson and vice chairperson
B. Committee chairpersons and vice chairpersons

Appointed Members:
C. Recording Secretary
D. Treasurer

Ex Officio Members:
E. Presiding officers of all parish organizations
F. Immediate last three chairpersons of the council

The pastor and associate pastor serve as nonvoting members of the council unless an issue receives an identical number of votes.

Section 2. Should an issue receive an identical number of votes, the pastor or his clerical representative will vote to break the tie.

Section 3. The vice chairperson of the council shall be elected by members of (name of parish).

Section 4. Each committee chairperson may appoint nonelected members to his or her committee. These members will be entitled to the full stature of elected council members except that they will serve in a nonvoting capacity.

Section 5. The pastor or his clerical representative shall serve as ex officio, nonvoting members of the council, except as stated in Article IV, Section 2.

Section 6. Should the position of chairperson of a committee become vacant, the vice chairperson shall automatically become chairperson for the unexpired term plus one subsequent term.

Should the position of vice chairperson of a committee become vacant, the committee chairperson shall appoint (subject to the approval of the council) an acting vice chairperson until the next election of the council.

Should the positions of both the chairperson and vice chairperson of a committee become vacant, the council chairperson shall appoint an acting chairperson and vice chairperson of the committee until the next election of the council. At the next election, both a chairperson and vice chairperson will be elected.

Section 7. If a member is absent for three consecutive meetings without good cause known, his or her name shall be removed from membership. A written notice of removal shall be sent to the person, who shall cease to be a member of the council.

Section 8. Any member of the council may resign by filing a written resignation with the recording secretary.

Section 9. As used within these bylaws, a "parishioner" is defined as any person who regularly attends (name of parish) and is registered on the parish roll.

ARTICLE V—ELECTIONS
Section 1. The council chairperson, with the advice of the council, shall appoint a nominating committee, which will be responsible for the nomination of council candidates and for the conduct of the election. The chairperson of the

nominating committee will be appointed by the council. The nominating committee shall consist of three parishioners who are not voting members of the council, and two parishioners who are voting members of the council.

The nominating committee will be appointed two months prior to the election.

At least one month prior to the election, the nominating committee shall distribute to parishioners a list of proposed candidates.

Installation Ceremony for Parish Pastoral Council

(Council members enter in procession with the priest. They take seats in the front pews. After the homily, the pastor invites the members of the parish pastoral council to come forward and stand in view of the congregation.)

Pastor: Will you make every effort to model your life on Jesus Christ, who is the source of our parish community life?
Candidates: We will.

Pastor: Will you dedicate the time, prayer, and study necessary to form a parish pastoral council in the spirit of the Second Vatican Council?
Candidates: We will.

Pastor: Will you do your utmost to promote the spiritual and material welfare of our parish, our diocese, and ultimately the world?
Candidates: We will.

Pastor: *(to congregation)* Are you willing to accept and support these pastoral council members in their prayerful deliberations and decisions for the good of the people of God?
All: We are.

Pastor: *(to congregation)* Let us give a sign of our acceptance and approval of these council members we have chosen.
All: *(applause to indicate approval)*

Pastor: We welcome you into leadership ministry in *(name of parish)*. We thank you for your willingness to serve. May God bless all your labors.
(Pastor congratulates and gives each member a parish pastoral council pin.)

Pastor: Let us pray… Lord God, look down upon us today and send forth your Spirit to bless, strengthen, and inspire these, your servants, who are offering a special ministry in our parish pastoral council. Help them be responsive to your Word, sensitive to the needs of others, and reconciling in their relationships. Give them the vision and courage to seek the truth and to discern your will in all matters they will be required to consider. Bestow upon them the grace to fulfill their roles in the mission of your Son.
All: Amen.
(Pastor invites council members to return to their seats.)

(I am indebted to Ministry Formation Services, Diocese of Nashville, for this installation ceremony.)

Section 2. Any parishioner who is qualified to serve as a member of the council but was not nominated by the nominating committee may have his or her name placed on the ballot by submitting to the council chairperson at least fifteen days prior to the election, a written request that his or her name be so placed on the ballot.

Section 3. Election ballots shall consist of at least three candidates for each committee:

Unit:	Minimum Number of Candidates:
Council Chairperson and/ or Vice Chairperson	3
Chairperson and/or Vice Chairperson of Administrative and Stewardship Committee	3
Chairperson and/or Vice Chairperson of Communications Committee	3
Chairperson and/or Vice Chairperson of Education & Formation Committee	3
Chairperson and/or Vice Chairperson of Family Life Committee	3
Chairperson and/or Vice Chairperson of Parish Life Committee	3
Chairperson and/or Vice Chairperson of Social Action Committee	3
Chairperson and/or Vice Chairperson of Worship and Spiritual Life Committee	3
Chairperson and/or Vice Chairperson of Missions Committee	3

Section 4. The annual election shall be held in the first two weeks of December. All elected officers of the council shall begin their terms of office on January 1 following the election.

Section 5. On January 1 after each annual election, the chairperson of each committee will retire and the vice chairperson will automatically become chairperson. All vice chair positions will then be filled according to the election.

All vacated positions as defined above and in Article IV, Section 6, will then be filled as a result of votes cast in the election as follows:

A. If positions of both chairperson and vice chairperson of a committee are vacant, parishioners will vote for two candidates. The candidate receiving the most votes shall become chairperson until the January following the next election, at which time he or she shall retire. The candidate receiving the next most number of votes shall become vice chairperson until the January following the next annual election, at which time he or she will automatically become chairperson of the committee.

B. If only the position of vice chairperson of a committee is vacant, parishioners will vote for one candidate. The candidate receiving the most votes shall be elected vice chairperson until the January following the next annual election, at which time he or she will become chairperson of the committee.

Section 6. Any parishioner at least 18 years of age is entitled to submit one ballot in the election of voting members.

ARTICLE VI—CONDUCT OF COUNCIL MEETINGS

Section 1. Council meetings shall be held at the principal office of the parish or a place designated by the chairperson or pastor.

Section 2. Council meetings shall be held monthly at a date and time designated by the council chairperson. All regular meetings shall be open to all parishioners, and notice of meetings shall be published in the church bulletin on the prior Sunday.

Section 3. Special council meetings may be called by the council chairperson or the pastor on three days notice given personally or by mail or telephone.

Section 4. The acts of the majority of the voting members at a council meeting at which a quorum is present shall be the acts of the council, except as otherwise stated herein.

Section 5. The council chairperson or vice chairperson shall preside at all council meetings and the recording secretary shall keep minutes of each meeting.

Section 6. Minutes of council meetings shall be available to all members of the parish.

Section 7. Records shall be kept of all committee meetings, and committee chairpersons shall report on his or her committee's activities to the council at regular meetings. In the absence of the committee chairperson, the committee vice chairperson or an appointed representative shall report on committee activities.

ARTICLE VII—RULES OF ORDER

Whenever an agenda item is presented for action at a meeting of a parish council or committee, members will attempt to reach a consensus after directed discussion. To obtain this objective, Rules of Order shall be maintained by the council chairperson in accordance with the following norms:

Section 1. The council chairperson may call for directed discussion, which shall proceed as follows: the chairperson will invite each member to address the question; members may pass until others have spoken; no one may speak twice until all have been given an opportunity to speak. After all have spoken, the chairperson may attempt to formulate a consensus of the council, with discussion continuing until

PARISH PASTORAL COUNCIL MISSION STATEMENT

As members of the parish pastoral council,
We will strive to love the Lord each day in our work, service, celebration, and prayers.

We will strive each day to see and to hear
Those who selected us as laypersons
To organize, interpret, and direct
Programs and actions of our parish
For the work of the Lord.

the chairperson has been able to formulate the final consensus and directs that this consensus be recorded in the council minutes.

Section 2. The council chairperson may permit free (nondirected) discussion until satisfied, with the consensus recorded in the minutes.

Section 3. Any member of the council has the right to propose that a particular meeting or portion of a meeting be conducted strictly in accordance with parliamentary procedure. Without permitting discussion of this proposal, the chairperson will call for a vote and, with a majority consenting, use *Robert's Rules of Order.*

Section 4. If any member makes a parliamentary motion at any time during any meeting with the words "I formally move" or their equivalent, the consideration of that motion and any amendments to it must be conducted in accordance with *Robert's Rules of Order.*

ARTICLE VIII—AMENDMENTS

Section 1. The council, by a consensus of its voting members, shall have the power to draft and amend these bylaws.

Section 2. Any amendments to these bylaws shall be communicated to the parish.

Section 3. Any parishioner desiring to express his or her difference of opinion toward any amendment made by the council to these bylaws, should come forward at the next meeting of the council and be duly heard.

Evaluation of Effectiveness of the Parish Pastoral Council

At the end of the church year circulate among council members a form for self-analysis, to be used in evaluating and improving effectiveness of the council. A suggested form for this purpose is reproduced on the next page.

On page 12 is a second form to be distributed among members of the general congregation. It, also, is designed to evaluate and improve effectiveness of the council.

PARISH PASTORAL COUNCIL SELF-ANALYSIS

Name of Committee: _____

How often did your committee meet? _____

1. What was the most important goal of your committee?

_____

    A. Do you feel your committee met this goal? ❏ Yes ❏ No

    B. If yes, list steps your committee took to meet the goal.

_____
_____
_____

    C. If no, list some of the reasons your committee failed to meet the goal.

_____
_____
_____

2. What was your second most important goal?

_____

A. Do you feel your committee met this goal?   ❏ Yes ❏ No

B. If yes, list steps your committee took to reach goal.

_____
_____
_____

C. If no, list some reasons why your committee failed.

_____
_____
_____

EVALUATION OF THE PARISH PASTORAL COUNCIL
ALL SAINTS CHURCH

1. On the whole, do you feel that the parish pastoral council has been effective this year?
❑ Yes   ❑ No

2. List a few of the programs or activities you feel have been most beneficial to the parish. (A few examples of programs: 10 o'clock Coffees, Shelter Program, Adopted Parish in Central America, Spiritual Retreats, Bible Study, Liturgy of the Word for Children, Picnic, Lending Library, Newsletter, Craft Fair, Nursery, Blood Drives, Habitat for Humanity, Meals on Wheels, Hospital Visitation program, Flower Ministry, Food Program.)

_____

_____

_____

_____

3. List a few of the programs or activities you feel have been of least benefit to All Saints Parish:

_____

_____

4. List names of a few members of the pastoral parish council:

_____

5. What should the parish pastoral council do to improve its service to All Saints Parish?

_____

_____

6. If asked to be a member of the council would you accept? ❑ Yes ❑ No ❑ Don't Know

7. (Optional) What are your interests, fields of expertise?

_____

_____   _____
Your Signature (optional)   Telephone Number (optional)

Chapter 2

Administration and Stewardship

Every parish needs someone to coordinate the efficient financial and administrative operation of the parish and to encourage stewardship among parishioners.

Committee Members

For this committee, seek out parishioners in fields of accounting, bookkeeping, banking, finance, law, insurance, investment counseling, security, fire prevention, personnel, employment services, CPAs, notary publics, and fund-raising. Consider administrators, office managers, and business people both active and retired.

Goals

• To coordinate expenditures of the parish.

• To educate and encourage parishioners in support of the church through stewardship of time, talent, and treasure.

• To account for parish properties and to provide guidance in property uses.

• To coordinate parish fund-raising programs.

• To conduct a complete census of the parish and to update this census on an ongoing basis.

• To formulate a program of personnel policies for the parish.

Objectives

• *To coordinate expenditures of the parish.*
1. Study tax exemption procedures. Your church should be listed as tax-exempt both by the federal government for gifts and donations, and by your state for the purpose of tax-exempt purchases. Be sure the state has assigned your church a tax-exempt number.

2. Assist parish groups and committees in preparing their annual budgets.
   A. Compile budgets from past years, budgets from committees of other parishes, and samples from publications related to church budgeting.
   B. Meet with each committee and ministry team to prepare estimates of annual expenditures, keeping in mind the overall goals and long-range needs of the parish.

3. Present budgets of committees to the Finance Board.
   A. Combine budget estimates from all committees.
   B. Prepare overall annual budget for both operating and capital expenditures, based on goals and objectives.
   C. Present budget for approval.

   Monitoring budgets of parish groups and

committees (i.e., reviewing expenditures vs. amounts budgeted) should be a regular task of the administration and stewardship committee. If such studies are conducted during the fiscal year, committees can make adjustments.

In this and other ways the administration and stewardship committee sees to the short-

---

THE FINANCE BOARD

Canon Law requires every parish to have a finance board, which is to exist separately and apart from the parish council. The board is not part of the administration and stewardship committee. Its members are appointed for three-year terms by the pastor in consultation with the parish council. A change of pastor has no effect on appointments.

The finance board assists the pastor in administration of financial assets of the parish.

Functions of the Finance Board:

1. To review and approve budgets of the parish groups as submitted by the administration and stewardship committee;

2. To prepare expense reports;

3. To review incoming money and expenditures of the parish to determine if the parish is operating wisely and within proper limits;

4. To help prepare a financial statement for submission to the chancery;

5. To make recommendations for increasing revenues, implementing pledges, developing endowments, soliciting wills and bequests;

6. To implement a pledge plan in the parish;

7. To study insurance needs.

(Much of this information is from Ministry Formation Services, Diocese of Nashville, TN.)

---

range financial matters of the parish. Long-range matters, however, are in the hands of the finance board.

• *To educate and encourage parishioners to support the church through stewardship of time, talent, and treasure.*

1. Study the Parish Stewardship Program as developed by the National Catholic Stewardship Council. The Liturgical Press in Collegeville, MN offers a Review Kit that has everything needed to begin the program.

2. Send a letter to parish members in which tithing and stewardship are emphasized. Include printed literature.

3. Promote tithing and stewardship through articles in parish newsletter, through displays and exhibits, and through literature made available to parishioners.

4. Promote Pledge Sunday.

• *To account for parish properties and to provide guidance in property use.*

1. Develop an inventory of all parish properties.

2. Keep inventory cards up to date. Use them to prepare an inventory (for insurance purposes) to be submitted to the finance board.

3. Study parish needs and advise on purchase or disposal of equipment, property, or facilities.

4. Submit a copy of the parish inventory to the pastoral council with cost estimates of anticipated maintenance, replacement, or repair.

5. Organize a building and grounds subcommittee and direct its operation.

6. Formulate policies regarding fire, safety, security, and provisions for the disabled.

7. Develop a systematic method for counting and processing church collections.

8. Develop teams of parishioners who will donate time and skills to:

    A. Attend to parish maintenance, including minor carpentry, repairs, and landscaping.

    B. Count and record church collections.

    C. Handle inventory and census procedures.

•To coordinate all parish fund-raising programs.

1. Assume responsibility for any capital or major fund campaign undertaken by the parish.

2. Request that all fund-raising programs be cleared through the administration and stewardship committee.

3. Review proposed fund-raising programs for feasibility, timing, and appropriateness.

4. Cooperate with fund-raisers to ensure careful receipt and accounting for monies.

•To conduct a complete parish census and to update this census on an ongoing basis.

•To formulate a program of personnel policies for the parish.

1. Assign job titles to all employees. Every worker deserves a named position. Rather than "doing work at the church," they should take pride in their jobs as housekeeper, cook, custodian, secretary, youth coordinator, etc.

2. Prepare job descriptions with salary ranges for all employees. Of course, everyone works together but, on a day-by-day basis, does the cook mop the kitchen? Does the custodian shop for groceries? Who answers the doorbell? Who looks after the laundry? Who schedules christenings, weddings, funerals? Who feeds the rectory's cat?

3. Prepare a list of personnel policies and procedures: office hours and work hours, break and lunch times, insurance, hospitalization, salary increases and deductions, pensions, book of days such as work days, sick days, leave days, pay days, off-without-pay days.

SPECIFIC PROJECTS IN DETAIL

Any Catholic church that is listed in the Official Catholic Directory is tax-exempt. This exemption is shared by organizations integral to the parish, as long as all expenditures go through parish books. If you want the full picture, here it is.

Tax Exemption Procedures

Form 1023 is a 30-page exercise issued by the Internal Revenue Service, which includes schedules for churches and schools. These procedures are listed:

1. Provide a brief history of the development of your organization, including the reasons for its formation.

2. If your organization has a written creed or statement of faith, attach a copy.

3. Does your organization require prospective members to renounce other religious beliefs or membership in other churches or religious orders to become members?

4. If your organization has a formal code of doctrine and discipline for its members, give a description of them.

The IRS points out that, because beliefs and practices vary widely, there is no single definition of the word "church" for tax purposes. The IRS considers the facts and circumstances of each organization.

A church is not required to file Form 1023 in order to be exempt from federal income tax or to receive tax deductible contributions, according to an IRS publication, "Tax-Exempt Status for Your Organization." However, a church may find it advantageous to obtain recognition of exemption.

It might be of interest to keep a copy of this publication in your church files, along with a companion booklet entitled "Application for Recognition of Exemption," which includes a copy of the formidable Form 1023.

Inventory of Parish Items

1. First, assign a number to each item. Affix the number to the item, using an indelible marker, an engraving pen, or a strip of marking tape. Then enter the number and the name of the item on a master inventory list.

2. Next, prepare an object card for each item. Include on the card the name of the object, the category, the object number, the source or vendor, the date of purchase or acquisition, cost or estimated value, warranty information, dates of servicing or replacement. In some cases it may be advisable to make a notation of the location of the item.

3. Set up an easily accessible file drawer for the object cards.

Arrange object cards alphabetically under such general classifications as:

Rectory Furnishings
   Examples: chairs, tables, lamps, mirrors, paintings, radio, television.

Kitchenware and Appliances
   Examples: washer and dryer, refrigerator, stove, microwave, dishwasher, pots and pans, china, glassware, silverware, cooking utensils.

Office Equipment
   Examples: desks and chairs, typewriter, copy machine, file cabinets,

telephones and answering devices, computer and printer.

Maintenance Supplies and Equipment
Examples: floor polishers, power mowers and lawn tools, vacuum cleaners, ladders, snow blowers.

Linens
Examples: window curtains or draperies, sheets, towels, pillows, blankets, tablecloths.

Books and Magazine Subscriptions
Examples: hymnals and missalettes. At the close of the fiscal year count them

and reorder as needed to keep a desired number on hand.

Sanctuary Furnishings, Linens, and Worship Aids
Examples: vesture for priest and choir, linens, liturgical objects and books, furniture, sacred images, paintings, collection plates, fonts, confessionals, kneelers that are not built in, flower containers.

Transportation
Examples: pastor's car, church bus, van, gospel buggy.

Annual Budgets

Parish committees and ministries should complete the basics before asking the Finance Board for assistance in budget preparation. After all, a committee best knows its own services and understands its own expenses. Study this sample budget.

ANNUAL BUDGET, COMMUNICATIONS COMMITTEE

(1) Quarterly Newsletter:
Estimated cost of printing
Four issues @ $325.00/each . . . .$ 1,300.00
Estimated cost of mailing, bulk rate, Four mailings @ $62.00/each 248.00

(2) Directory
Estimated cost of printing 2,000 copies 250.00

(3) Monthly Calendar (Reproduced on photocopy machine)
Cost of paper (12 packages @ $6.00/each) 72.00

(4) Newcomer Packets
Estimated cost of printing 289.00

(5) Scrapbook (Cost of binder, materials) 40.00

(6) Photographs for scrapbook, display board, cost of film, photo finishing 60.00

(7) Literature rack (Cost of metal rack) 50.00

(8) Family Bookshelf, Estimated cost of 25–30 basic books 400.00

TOTAL . . . .$ 2,709.00

In some parishes certain expenses, such as the cost of the newsletter or the church directory, are covered under the general fund.

Sample: Creating a Master Inventory

Give each item a number and enter in a Master Inventory List:

MASTER INVENTORY, ALL SAINTS CHURCH

Object Number:	Item:
1	Refrigerator
2	Upright Freezer
3	Stove
4	Microwave Oven
5 a-f	Mixer with bowls and attachments
6 a-e	Vacuum Cleaner with attachments
7 a-p	16-piece Silverware, Fiddle Leaf Pattern
8 a-y	25-piece China, Apple Blossom Pattern
9 a-t	20-piece Crystal, Omega Pattern
10 a-e	Coffee Service with Tray
11	Hall Table
12	Hall Mirror, 40" X 60"
13	Carpet Runner, 3' X 20'
14	Coat/Hat Rack
15 a-d	Four Parlor Chairs, Queen Anne Style
16	Sofa, Queen Anne Style
17	Pie Crust Table
18	Refectory Table
19	Coffee Table
20	Oil Painting, All Saints Church ca 1910
21	Watercolor, The Wicked Flea
22	Parlor Carpet 20' X 30'
23	Floor Lamp with Shade
24	Table Lamp with Shade

The Object Card. 4" X 5" is the most feasible size.

INVENTORY CARD, ALL SAINTS CHURCH

Category: Kitchenware & Appliances   **Object Number:** 1

Object: Westinghouse Refrigerator, Model 38-B

Description: Top Freezer, ice maker, crisper, Warranty # 5448-A

How Acquired (Purchase/Gift/Loan): Purchase

Date Acquired: 10/27/93   **Cost or Est. Value:** $780.00

Vendor: Brown's Appliance Service, Telephone 298-3397

Be selective in marking articles for the church inventory. Do not include such expendable items as groceries, cleaning materials, personal articles, or objects that do not belong to the parish.

Building and Grounds Subcommittee

Under the direction of the administration and finance committee, the building and grounds subcommittee is given charge of repair and maintenance, safety and security, and provisions for the disabled.

1. Buildings:

A. Supervise church custodian, janitor, work crews.

B. Seek out the most feasible method of solid waste disposal. If your church discards more than two cubic yards of refuse each week (that's eight 55-gallon drums full) consider renting a front-loader container. Costs vary but plan on at least $50/week for this service.

C. Attend to minor painting and repairs, alert administration and stewardship committee of needed major expenses.

D. Assume responsibility for storage and setup of needed furniture and equipment, such as tables and folding chairs.

E. Assume responsibility for installation and weekly updates of outdoor bulletin board.

2. Grounds:

A. Seed, water, mow, weed, and rake grassy areas; plant, water, weed, and feed flower beds and borders.

B. Work with worship and spiritual life committee in maintaining flower beds and borders, grottoes, exterior shrines, and outdoor Stations of the Cross.

C. Maintain walls, walks, and parking areas. (1) See to paving and repairing of parking area, apply seal coating to asphalt every three years.

Outdoor Bulletin Boards

Changeable-letter boards are available from most church supply firms or display companies at prices ranging from $500 to $7,000. A lot depends on size, lighting, locking, and labor. Some churches prefer electronic boards. Prices for electronic boards range from $5,000 to $10,000 (and up).

Before you invest in an outdoor bulletin board take a few moments to consider the commitment involved. A sign-changer must post messages each week, usually while perched atop a ladder. Days can be hot, cold, windy, or wet. A double-faced sign means double work. However, millions of churches feel this ministry is well worth the effort.

The average 2 X 3-foot changeable letter board has room for up to 36 lines, approximately 50 characters per line. In addition to information about Masses and meetings, many churches post additional material, such as the responsorial psalm for that Sunday or a thought-provoking one-liner. Work with the communications committee in preparing weekly copy for the outdoor bulletin board.

(2) Attend to lining asphalt for parking. In marking spaces bear in mind that the average automobile requires at least 9 X 18 feet, a bit more length if parking space is at an angle. An additional 24 feet is required to back and turn. Two-way lanes should be at least 24 feet wide. Spaces should be marked with a yellow or white weather resistant paint that adheres to asphalt. It is best if lines are painted by a commercial firm. Seek Yellow Pages listings under Paving Contractors, Parking, or Pavement Marking Services.

If your parish needs property for additional parking, figure that a lot approximately 70 X 150 feet in size will provide about 28 parking spaces.

(3) Make provision for handicap parking. Appropriate stencils can be obtained from American Stencil, West 28 Washington Avenue, Pearl River, NY 10965. Large plastic wall signs are available at hardware supply stores.

(4) If your parish operates a bus, provide a loading area for the disabled near the church entrance.

(5) Attend to ice/snow removal on steps, walkways, parking areas.

D. Assume responsibility for parish vehicles including maintenance and repair, registration, licensing, insurance coverage, screening and supervising drivers.
By definition, a passenger bus is a vehicle that carries at least nine persons and a driver.
Most states have rules and regulations for vehicles classified as church buses: the vehicle can be painted any color other than yellow (reserved for school vehicles) but must be identified as a church bus. Most states require flashing lights on the roof, red and amber on each side (red on the outside). Seat belts are required if the bus carries fewer than 15 passengers. The church must carry a minimum $500,000 insurance for bodily injury and property damage. The driver must have a chauffeur's license. There is a growing tendency to require an assistant to the driver.

Duties You May Expect from a Church Security Guard

A. Patrol the area.

B. Discourage loitering, littering, or loud/unruly behavior.

C. Prohibit use of alcohol or controlled substances.

D. Prohibit vehicles from parking in unauthorized places.

E. If necessary, control street traffic for benefit of vehicles exiting the parking lot.

F. Guards may be asked to perform other duties from time to time, such as:

(1) Assist handicapped persons with wheelchairs;

(2) Summon road service for those with disabled vehicles;

(3) Effect rescues for persons with keys locked in vehicles;

(4) Check vehicle lights, especially on rainy days;

(5) Offer umbrella escort;

(6) Upon request, provide safety escort between church and parking area.

Your church may feel that a conveyance is needed to transport elderly/disabled parishioners from car to church door. An electric golf cart is ideal for such a "Gospel Buggy." Your parish membership probably includes a retired golfer who would be willing to donate a cart. Seek a cart that seats at least four and features an awning for protection against sun and rain. Remember that the cart's home base will need electricity for recharging.

Fire, Safety, and Security

1. Inspect church property on a regular basis for possible fire violations or safety hazards.

2. See that maps are posted outlining fire escape routes, and that all exits are kept clear and free of obstructions.

3. Consider a Sunday sentry if buildings are in an unsafe area or if parishioners are frequently confronted by strangers on church property.

Hire a security guard or engage an off-duty police officer for the job. Be aware that security guards are not qualified as police officers. However, they have received special training, have undergone fingerprint checks, and, in most states, have met other requirements for state registration as security guards. Police officers in most communities are allowed to accept freelance assignments on their off-duty hours.

4. For the safety of the parish staff and the security of church property, check out the benefits of an electronic surveillance system. Closed-circuit cameras, placed at entrances and in the sanctuary, are connected to a monitor in the church office. The sanctuary thus can be kept under observation and visitors can be identified at the entrance. Many systems offer an optional "med-alert button" to summon medical assistance.

Many people will say, with some justification, that a church should be open at all times. Sadly, this is not always wise, but each parish will need to make its own decision.

Provisions for the Disabled

Certain requirements have been established by the American Disability Act (ADA). At this writing, for example, at least one entrance to a public building must be equipped with a ramp for wheelchairs, with slope not to exceed 1 to 12 inches (example, one-inch rise for every twelve inches of length). The ramp must be at least 44 inches wide with a handrail 34 inches high.

In places of assembly with fixed seating, accessible wheelchair locations shall be provided consistent with the following table:

Capacity of Seating in Assembly Areas	Number of Required Wheelchair Locations
4 to 25	1
26 to 50	2
51 to 300	4
301 to 500	6

Reserve special spaces in the parking area for the handicapped, mark them, and encourage parishioners to observe the rules.

A full review of provisions for the disabled is available from the U.S. Architectural and Transportation Barriers Compliance Board, 1331 F Street, NW, Suite 1000, Washington, DC 20004-1111.

Provisions for the Hearing Impaired

To accommodate the totally deaf, reserve seats close to the ambo and lectern for benefit of lip readers. Some churches recruit signers to stand before the congregation to act as interpreters. If a person appears at church leading a dog with an orange harness, the animal probably is a trained Hearing Ear dog, allowed by most laws to travel with its deaf master.

For the benefit of the hearing impaired, a parish can choose from three basic types of assistive listening devices:

A. The FM Broadcast system, probably the most popular, which requires a central transmitter and individual receivers. The cost: $400 and up for transmitters, approximately $85 each for receivers. Installation is nontechnical.

B. The Sound TV Infrared System, which requires a transmitter and individual receivers, but which can be tied in with existing PA systems. The cost: about the same as FM systems. Transmission will not travel through solid surfaces, so seated users might lose sound if persons around them stand.

C. The Induction Loop System, in which an amplifier drives an induction loop surrounding the listening area. Signals can be received by individual receivers (approximately $85 each) or by personal hearing aids equipped with a telecoil. Installation involves placement of loop wire, which may be difficult in pre-existing buildings.

Provisions for the Visually Impaired

Include large-print, Braille, and recorded versions of books in the parish library. Place Braille plates on elevators. Keep all areas well lighted. Note that most state laws allow Seeing Eye dogs in public buildings.

Count Money and Record Church Collections

(This procedure is adapted from a plan by Anne Greene Rolman of Nashville, TN.)

Suggested supplies/equipment: adding machine with printout tape, coin wrappers, envelopes, access to a photocopying machine.

A team consists of a captain and assistants. For protection of teams and treasure, at least two persons should be with monies at all times. If there are two collections, process them separately. Sort money into loose checks, loose cash, and church envelopes.

I. Loose Checks:

1. Process loose checks as follows:

    A. List checks (name and amount) on form as indicated.

    B. Use adding machine to run tape-listing of check list and checks. The two tape totals should agree.

    C. Make photocopy of checks and of log.

    Keep checks in same order as photocopies.

    D. Endorse checks.

    E. Band original checks and photocopies, log, and photocopy with adding machine tape. Mark tape "Loose checks," with date and time of Mass.

2. Team captain enters figures on Totals Forms.

II. Loose Cash:

1. Process loose cash as follows:

    A. Separate bills by denomination and sort into bundles of $50, $100, $500. All bills should face same direction. A second team member recounts to verify.

    B. Place coins in coin wrappers. Place excess coins in envelope; write amount on envelope.

    C. Fill out form listing total coins of each denomination and total amount of coins, total bills of each denomination, and total amount. Total coins plus total bills equal total cash received.

D. Repeat procedure for cash from envelopes. Run tape-listing for each category: church pledge, education, Peter's Pence, Mission. Run tape-listing of envelopes, by category. Totals should agree.

2. Team captain enters figures on Totals Forms.

III. Church Envelopes:

1. Separate envelopes by color.

Envelopes include: church pledges (usually gold), Peter's Pence (yellow), Mission (green), Catholic Communications (tan), Parish (white), Education (pink).

A. Open envelopes. Put cash and checks in separate stacks.

B. Mark on front of envelope the dollar amount and form (cash or check). Envelopes with cash and envelopes with checks should be kept separate.

2. For envelopes containing checks: If there are multiple checks in one envelope mark each dollar amount on the envelope. If there is one check accompanied by several envelopes (and all envelopes are the same color) write the amount of the check on one of the envelopes and destroy the others. If there is one check covering two charities with a second envelope, mark dollar amounts on parish envelope and clip the second envelope to it. Write information on paper slip and place in appropriate stack.

A. Stack envelopes, flaps closed, in same order as checks.

B. On adding machine, run tape-listing of checks designated for the parish. Run tape-listing of envelopes. Totals should agree. Enter total amount on collection form.

C. Run tape-listing of checks designated for categories other than parish by categories; run tape-listing of envelopes by categories. Totals should agree. Enter amount on collection form.

D. Endorse checks.

E. Band envelopes (by color) and checks with adding machine tape. Mark "Envelopes: checks" and enter date and time of Mass.

3. For envelopes containing cash: Turn envelopes with contents over to team member in charge of loose cash.

A. Remove cash. Mark envelope "Cash" and write the dollar amount if this has not been done.

B. Run tape on envelopes. Run tape on cash received. Totals should agree. After adding totals, mingle cash with loose cash.

C. Band cash envelopes (by color) with machine tape. Mark "Envelopes: cash" and enter date and time of Mass.

4. Team captain enters figures on Totals Forms.

Before you Finalize Your Procedure

Visit the head teller at your bank. Ask about bank requirements. For example, are adding machine tapes to be included with deposits? Should full rolls of coins be sealed with tape? How should half-rolls be handled? When is the best time to make a bank deposit?

ALL SAINTS CHURCH
REPORT OF COLLECTIONS

(Date) _____

❑ First Collection   ❑ Second Collection   ❑ Other Collection

Cash Received:

Coins:.   .01 $ _____

.05 _____

.10 _____

.25 _____

.50 _____

1.00 _____

+ _____

Total Coins: $ _____

Bills: 1.00 $ _____

2.00 _____

5.00 _____

10.00 _____

20.00 _____

50.00 _____

+ _____

Total Bills: $ _____

* Checks Received: $ _____

+ _____

Total Collection: $ _____

* List checks on separate sheet (see page 25), enter total.

ALL SAINTS CHURCH
LISTING OF CHECKS RECEIVED

Name of Contributor: Amount:

_____ $ _____

_____ $ _____

_____ $ _____

_____ $ _____

_____ $ _____

_____ $ _____

_____ $ _____

_____ $ _____

_____ $ _____

_____ $ _____

_____ $ _____

_____ $ _____

_____ $ _____

_____ $ _____

_____ $ _____

_____ $ _____

_____ $ _____

_____ $ _____

_____ $ _____

_____ $ _____

Total Amount of Checks: $ _____

Fund-Raising Programs

Eventually, your parish will become involved in a major fund campaign. The roof may go, lack of space may make an addition necessary, storm or fire could bring heavy structural damage, or you could decide it's time for extensive renovation or a new location.

Before you begin, get in touch with parishes that have conducted successful campaigns and ask for tips and suggestions. Ask for advice from your diocesan office. Seek out books on fund-raising—four suggestions from the scores that are available: *Fund Raising for Non Profit Groups* by L. Peter Edles (McGraw-Hill); *The Capital Campaign Handbook* by David J. Hauman (Taft Group); *The Raising of Money* by James Gregory Lord (Third Sector Press); *Fund Raising Guide to Religious Philanthropy* by

---

Companies that Can Help

Many companies offer help in needs assessment surveys, feasibility studies, and fund campaigns. Among them are the American City Bureau, Chicago; Hank Brandt Associates, Tucson, AZ; Community Counseling Service, John B. Cummings Company, and Martin J. Moran Company in New York City; Development Direction Inc., Mineola, NY; Harvey Fund-Raising Management, Inc., Milwaukee, WS; Kirby-Smith Associates, Quarryville, PA; John V. McCarthy & Associates, Southfield, MI; and Ruotolo Associates, Englewood, NJ. Addresses of most firms are in the Catholic Directory.

Bernard Jankowski (Taft Group). Also, check out professional fund-raising agencies. If your goal is $1 million or more your church probably should consider engaging a consultant.

Be forewarned: Planning and preliminaries will take time, perhaps a year or more, but careful action at this point might determine the success of your campaign.

The strength and sinew of every fund-raising effort is a steering committee or campaign cabinet, made up of eight to eighteen carefully chosen parishioners. The over-used term "movers and shakers" comes to mind. Essential at this point are persons of strength, power, knowledge, dedication, and commitment.

Members of the steering committee should be prepared to evaluate policies, approve procedures, speak publicly on behalf of the campaign, identify and solve any major problems, enlist additional campaign leaders, and approach key persons or groups for lead gifts. In addition, they should be prepared to make their own personal gift to the campaign.

The first step in planning is an assessment of the current financial needs of your parish and, more complex, an assessment of your capacity to meet these needs.

Begin the needs assessment process by adding all needs and expenses that will make up the goal of the fund campaign. For example, if a new building or wing has been proposed, itemize the total cost of construction as submitted by your contractor. Sometimes overlooked is the fact that a new building will require new furnishings and equipment. Obtain cost estimates for such items and add to your anticipated needs. A new building also will probably mean an increase in insurance premiums, a higher cost of electricity or other utilities. If construction is involved, allow for the expense of permits, legal fees, moving and drayage. Finally, remember to include in your needs the expense of the fund drive itself.

The capacity of your parish to meet these financial needs is determined by the capability of your members and their commitment, their skill and dedication as campaign workers, and the time and resources that are available. Estimate this capacity by recording your parish's accomplishments for the year on the checklist on the following page.

CAMPAIGN BUDGET EXPENSES
Items to be remembered in your list of campaign expenses are:
- Salaries, FICA, insurance
- Printing: forms, envelopes
- Printing: pamphlets/folders
- Rent/Lease: office/equipment
- Office supplies/photocopies
- Telephone
- Postage: letters/newsletters
- Meeting expenses
- Travel expense, maintenance
- Audiovisuals/photography

CHECKLIST: PARISH CAPACITY

Does your parish set a dollar goal each year?
    ❑ Yes   ❑ No

Does your parish exceed its goal each year?
    ❑ Yes   ❑ No

Do you have a method to recognize major donors?
    ❑ Yes   ❑ No

Do you make at least four attempts to renew each previous donation?
    ❑ Yes   ❑ No

Is your campaign report system accurate and prompt?
    ❑ Yes   ❑ No

Are your donor records updated on a regular basis?
    ❑ Yes   ❑ No

Do you know the most productive zip codes?
    ❑ Yes   ❑ No

Are gifts made by members of your parish pastoral council?
    ❑ Yes   ❑ No

Do your parish council members cultivate donors and solicit gifts?
    ❑ Yes   ❑ No

Do members of your congregation support a fund campaign by making suggestions and providing leads?
    ❑ Yes   ❑ No

Does your parish have the time and staff necessary for a capital fund campaign?
    ❑ Yes   ❑ No

Feasibility Study

A feasibility study is the first step in deciding if your parish is ready for a capital campaign. The study seeks to determine if the time is right for a campaign and, if so, how much can be raised, if campaign leadership can be found, and what should be done to make the campaign a success. Generally speaking, the information is gained from one-on-one interviews with community leaders, your church leaders, past pastors, and selected diocesan personnel. It frequently happens that the persons interviewed make initial gifts or volunteer for leadership roles in the campaign.

Unless the amount needed is small you probably should engage an accredited fundraising consultant to handle the feasibility study and campaign.

Interviewers with training and experience are best able to get honest and unbiased answers. Select an objective agency that has no connection or affiliation with your parish. Remember that all answers must be kept confidential.

On the following pages you will find examples of materials that might be used in conducting a parish feasibility study. (This material is adapted from *The Manual for Financial Development: Fund Raising Made Easy*, courtesy of the American Red Cross. All Rights Reserved in all countries.) Included here are:

A. Letter from the pastor requesting names of key persons to be interviewed;

B. Letter from the pastor confirming an interview appointment;

C. Four-page guide for the interviewer conducting the feasibility study.

All Saints Church
706 Mary Street
Farley, IL 60201

Dr. J. P. Morgan, IV
President, City Bank
1111 Main Street
Farley, Illinois 22280

Dear Jay:

At All Saints Church we are planning a Feasibility Study to decide if the parish and the community will support a Capital Fund Campaign for a needed education building.

I am asking you and a few other members of our pastoral council to assist by providing ten names of members of the parish who (1) are in a position to make significant donations, (2) are in a position to influence donations by other parishioners, organizations, or businesses, or (3) are in a position to influence the campaign.

Send your list by November 1 to Douglas O'Neal, Chairman, Feasibility Studies. A stamped, addressed envelope is enclosed for your convenience.

A committee will review all information and will select persons to be interviewed. In the meantime, I ask you not to discuss this project because it is considered confidential.

Thank you for your assistance.

Sincerely,

Father Robert Blair
Pastor, All Saints Church
Encl.

All Saints Church
706 Mary Street
Farley, Illinois 60201

Mrs. Lydia Ladd, President
Illinois Foods, Inc.
195 Main Street
Farley, Illinois 60201

Dear Mrs. Ladd:

Thank you for agreeing to take part in the Feasibility Study for All Saints Church. Your appointment is scheduled at 10:30 A.M. on Friday, October 22, and will take place in your office. To best assure neutrality the interview will be conducted by a person not connected with All Saints Church, Mrs. Jane Jackson. As you know, this study will focus on a possible expansion program for All Saints. As an opinion leader, your input will be of great value to us.

I enclose three documents for you to study before meeting with Mrs. Jackson: (1) a Case Statement, which provides information about All Saints Church and its needs, (2) a presentation of our proposed goal, with levels of gifts needed to meet it, (3) a listing of potential major donors.

We ask that you look over this material and indicate, without divulging any confidences, what you think these donors would give, and who might approach them. Also, please list other persons we might approach for donations.

Your input will be held in strict confidence.

Mrs. Jackson will pick up this information when she meets with you.

Thank you for your cooperation.

Sincerely,

Father Robert Blair
Pastor, All Saints Church
Encl.

ALL SAINTS CATHOLIC CHURCH
INTERVIEW GUIDE FOR FEASIBILITY STUDY

Person interviewed: _____

Title/Position: _____

Company/Agency _____

Part I. All Saints Parish and the town of Farley, Illinois:

A. In your opinion, to what extent is the community of Farley involved in church and religious programs?

❑ Much involved   ❑ Normally involved   ❑ Little involved

B. How do you describe the economy of Farley?

❑ Stable   ❑ Growing   ❑ Declining   ❑ Verging on change

C. Name the two most active churches in Farley.

_____

D. To which organization, if any, have you contributed money during the past twelve months?

❑ American Cancer Society ❑ Heart Association
❑ American Red Cross ❑ Arthritis Foundation
❑ Boy/Girl Scouts ❑ Easter Seal Society
❑ All Saints Parish ❑ Parish other than All Saints
❑ YMCA/YWCA ❑ Other (name):_____

E. If you checked any organizations above, explain why you support them:

_____

F. Of the agencies listed above, in your opinion, which ones give the greatest return for your donated dollar?

_____

G. What comes to mind when you hear the name, "All Saints Parish"?

_____

H. What do you especially like about All Saints Parish?

_____

I. What do you dislike about All Saints Parish?

_____

J. What All Saints Parish programs have you seen or heard about during the past year?

_____

K. Are you familiar with any members of the All Saints Parish pastoral council?

❑ Yes ❑ No ❑ Not sure

If answer is "No" or "Not sure," interviewer should name a few council members, then repeat the question.

If answer is "Yes," interviewer should ask: "How does leadership of All Saints Parish compare with leadership in our overall community?"

❑ Better   ❑ About the same   ❑ Not as good

L. Have you ever been asked to serve as a team member, a committee member, or as a volunteer worker for All Saints Parish?

❑ Yes   ❑ No

If answer is yes, interviewer should ask, "In what capacity?"_____

If answer is no, interviewer should ask, "Would you respond if someone asked you?"

❑ Yes   ❑ No

If answer is no, interviewer should ask, "Why?" *If answer is "too busy," interviewer should ask,* "Would you serve at a later time?"   ❑ Yes   ❑ No

Part II. Giving to All Saints Catholic Church:

A. Where does All Saints Parish stand in your priority of financial support?

❑ Top Priority   ❑ Middle Priority   ❑ Low Priority

B. Have you given to All Saints Parish during the past year?

❑ Yes   ❑ No

C. In your opinion, what is the average amount given (annually) to All Saints Parish?

$ _____.

D. In your opinion, how does this compare with the average amount given to other churches in the Farley community?

❑ More than other churches   ❑ Less than other churches   ❑ About the same   ❑ Don't know

E. How would you describe the financial situation of All Saints Parish?

❑ Suffers from a serious fund shortage   ❑ Has minimum funds   ❑ Has adequate money
❑ Enjoys surplus funds   ❑ Don't know

F. Do you think a new education building/renovation is needed by All Saints Parish?

❑ Yes   ❑ No   ❑ Don't know

G. In a Capital Funds Campaign, do you think All Saints Parish could raise:

❑ $1,000,000   ❑ $500,000   ❑ $250,000   ❑ $125,000   ❑ $60,000

H. Would you be willing to contribute to All Saints Parish this year <u>without</u> a fund campaign?

❑ Yes Amount $ _____   ❑ No

Part III. All Saints Parish and Service to the Community:

A. I will now read a list of programs provided or supported by All Saints Parish. Please rate them as "Important," "Unimportant," or "Don't know."

	Important	Unimportant	Don't Know
Adopted Parish in Haiti	q	q	q
Room in the Inn Family Shelter	q	q	q
St. Patrick Shelter Program	q	q	q
"Loaves & Fishes" Food Program	q	q	q
Sandwiches for the Hungry	q	q	q
Literacy Program	q	q	q
Crisis Pregnancy	q	q	q
St. Vincent de Paul Program	q	q	q
Visits to the Homebound	q	q	q
Hospital Visitation	q	q	q
Aid to Burned-Out Families	q	q	q

B. On which programs do you think All Saints Parish spends the most money?

q Adopted Parish in Haiti
q Room in the Inn Family Shelter
q St. Patrick Shelter Program
q "Loaves & Fishes" Food Program
q Sandwiches for the Hungry
q Literacy Program
q Crisis Pregnancy
q St. Vincent de Paul Program
q Visits to the Homebound
q Hospital Visitation
q Aid to Burned-Out Families

C. In your opinion, whom does All Saints Parish serve in our community?

_____

D. Whom do you think All Saints Parish should serve?

_____

E. In your opinion, what are the strengths and weaknesses of All Saints Parish?

_____

F. In your opinion, what needs are not being met in our community?

_____

Do you think All Saints Parish could meet any of these needs?
       q Yes   q No

G. Are you supportive of assistance programs provided by All Saints Parish to:
❑ Those in the inner city
❑ Those in Third World countries
❑ The hungry through food programs
❑ The homeless through shelter programs
❑ Emigrants through literacy and settlement programs
❑ The homebound/elderly through visitation programs
❑ The handicapped through visitation programs
❑ The sick/injured/hospitalized through visitation programs
❑ Crisis pregnancy mothers
❑ Battered spouses

H. If lack of money forced All Saints Parish to decide between raising funds or cutting services, which course would you recommend?
　　　❑ Launch a fund campaign
　　　❑ Cut services

I. How can All Saints Parish improve its services to our community?

_____
_____
_____
_____
_____
_____
_____
_____
_____

This Interview was conducted by:
_____

Date of
Interview_____

Examine information from the feasibility study. It should tell you if a campaign is advisable, if donors sympathize with your need, if obstacles exist, and if leadership is available.

Phases of the Capital Campaign

In a capital campaign a significant part of the total goal comes from a small number of key donors, in fact, 40 to 50 percent of the goal should be received from such donors before the public kick-off. With this in mind, the wise steering committee will break the campaign into at least three phases: Initial Gifts (really big money), Advance Gifts (large amounts), and, after the campaign kickoff, Special Gifts. Pledges can be broken into payments over a period of three to five years.

Workers should make appointments with

THREE-YEAR GIFT PAYMENT PLAN

Gift	Payment	Balance	Monthly	Annually
$5,000	$ 500	$4,500	$ 125.00	$1,500.00
4,000	400	3,600	100.00	1,200.00
3,000	300	2,700	75.00	900.00
2,500	250	2,250	62.50	750.00
2,000	200	1,800	50.00	600.00
1,200	120	1,080	30.00	360.00

FOUR-YEAR GIFT PAYMENT PLAN

Gift	Payment	Balance	Monthly	Annually
$5,000	$ 500	$4,500	$ 93.75	$1,125.00
4,000	400	3,600	75.00	900.00
3,000	300	2,700	56.25	675.00
2,500	250	2,250	46.88	562.50
2,000	200	1,800	37.50	450.00
1,200	120	1,080	22.50	270.00

FIVE-YEAR GIFT PAYMENT PLAN

Gift	Payment	Balance	Monthly	Annually
$5,000	$ 500	$4,500	$ 75.00	$900.00
4,000	400	3,600	60.00	720.00
3,000	300	2,700	45.00	540.00
2,500	250	2,250	37.50	450.00
2,000	200	1,800	30.00	360.00
1,200	120	1,080	18.00	216.00

Initial Gift and Advance Gift prospects to deliver Campaign Donor Packets and review them.

Contents of Donor Packets

Letter from the pastor, the Case Statement, Questions and Answers, brochures about the campaign, an individual pledge card, and a suggested payment schedule.

1. The pastor's letter personalizes the appeal and indicates church commitment.

2. The Case Statement presents the background, states the problem, outlines the solution, explains the cost, and makes the challenge. It is the most important document in your support material.

> Review your parish's history. Describe its services. Emphasize its integrity and competence.

> Refer to your feasibility study and use results to link the project with interests of your donors.

> Explain the need. If you seek funding for a new building, for example, describe the present building and explain why it is no longer adequate.

> Explain the costs. If you are seeking money for renovation and repair, for example, present the expense in easily understood categories. If the appeal is for a new building, include sketches and floor plans, and explain proposed use of space.

3. Devote at least a full page to questions and answers.

> Suggested questions:

> A. "How did you decide on the amount I was asked to give?"

> B. "What if I can't fulfill my pledge?"

> C. "Exactly how will my money be used?"

4. The brochure is the "sales piece" of the campaign. It should include basic facts and figures, with sketches and photographs as needed. Parishioners will refer to it often as they discuss and think about the campaign.

5. The Pledge Card (see page 38) is printed in three sections, each section bearing the prospect's name, address, and telephone number.

> Visitors detach *section A* to give to their team captains as teams leave the assignment meeting.

> Team visitors retain *section B* after the pledge is made, to be sent to the campaign office.

> *Section C* remains with the parishioner.

A Campaign Donor Packet is assembled for each parishioner and placed in a manila envelope that is marked with the parishioner family's name.

Important Details of the Campaign

•During their visit, the team reviews the need, explains the campaign, and appeals for a commitment. Each prospect is asked to make an initial payment of ten percent, to be included with his or her pledge card.

•It should be noted that a capital campaign is designed to raise funds for a specific purpose, such as a major renovation or a new building.

Funds raised in a capital campaign are legally restricted and cannot be used for any other purpose.

•In preparation for your Special Gifts Campaign kickoff, assemble forms, supplies (including donor packets), and support material. Prepare a campaign donor packet for each prospect.

•Put together a schedule to coordinate the overall campaign to insure that materials will be printed on time, and to see that each phase of the campaign is completed according to schedule. For example, allow adequate time to recruit, orient, and assign leaders and workers, prepare and print materials, plan and schedule meetings, keep records, and prepare reports.

•Your campaign staff should include a capable computer operator to handle much of this work.

•Every experienced fund-raiser gives this caution: Do not kick off the public campaign too soon. First, evaluate progress of Initial and Advance Gifts. Adjust the goal, the schedule, or even the overall plan if necessary.

•Announce the results of these important phases of the drive at the kickoff of the Fund Campaign. It is to be hoped that you can say you *already* have achieved 40 to 50 percent of the goal!

•Prepare for the kickoff by recruiting team captains (one for each *ten* home-visit teams). At

The Pledge Card

BUILDING FUND CAMPAIGN ALL SAINTS CHURCH	BUILDING FUND CAMPAIGN ALL SAINTS CHURCH	BUILDING FUND CAMPAIGN ALL SAINTS CHURCH
Section A (Team Captain)	Section B (Church Office)	Section C (Parishioner)
Name: _____	Name:_____	Name:_____
Address: _____	Address:_____	Address:_____
City/State/Zip: _____	City/State/Zip:_____	City/State/Zip:_____
Telephone: _____	Telephone Number:_____	Amount of Pledge: $_____
Suggested Pledge: $_____	Suggested Pledge:_____	Amount of Down Payment $_____
Names of Visiting Team: _____ _____	Amount of Pledge:_____	Please bill me: ❏ Annually
	Down Payment (attached)_____	❏ Semiannually ❏ Quarterly for _____ years, ending 19/20____
	Please bill me: ❏ Annually	Names of Visiting Team Members:
	❏ Semiannually ❏ Quarterly for _____years, ending 19/20___	_____
	_____ (signature) (date)	_____
	Names of Visiting Team Members: _____ _____	

the first training meeting of the captains, explain the campaign (using charts, diagrams, printed materials). It is important that every worker be committed to the campaign.

• Explain the plan. Develop enthusiasm. Outline duties: Each captain should recruit at least ten two-member teams of home visitors (visits are best made in twos).

• After allowing time for captains to recruit their teams, schedule orientation/training sessions.

• See that teams understand the need, the plan, and the obligation.

• Each pair of visitors should agree to call on from five to ten families. At the close of the training meeting give the workers a list of families to be visited with pledge amounts to be sought. A suggested form is printed at right.

• Discuss ways of dealing with various types of people, different reactions to pledge requests, and the variety of questions they may be asked about the campaign. Review questions and answers. Involve workers in role play.

• At orientation/training sessions, distribute supplies in time for captains and team members to review and discuss. Urge workers to attend report meetings with team captains.

• Each campaign donor packet is printed with the name of the person or family to be visited.

• Should you include a suggested gift amount? Many potential donors resent being told what to give, but fund-raisers usually think it neces-

---

ALL SAINTS PARISH FUND CAMPAIGN

Names of Visiting Team:

_____

FAMILIES TO BE VISITED:

- -

Name: Mr. and Mrs. Hubert B. Herbert
Address: 14-B Tennis Court Drive
Tel. Number: 555-1414
Date of Visit: _____
 Amount of Pledge: $ 1,000.00

- -

Name: Dr. Paul N. Silas, III
Address: 259 Nevada Street, S.W.
Tel. Number: 555-6604
Date of Visit: _____
Amount of Pledge: $ 850.00

- -

Name: Ms. Ima Goodshoes
Address: Bellevue Apartments, # D-28
Tel. Number: 555-5990
Date of Visit: _____
Amount of Pledge: $ 1,500.00

- -

Name: Mrs. Gwen Grant Grosvenor
Address: 766 S. Seashore Street
Tel. Number: 555-7667
Date of Visit: _____
Amount of Pledge: $ 3,000.00

sary. The agency conducting your campaign will establish the amounts to be requested.

• There are many types of gifts: cash or check (which can be made in one payment or pledged over a period of several years), real estate, stocks, bonds, securities, wills, bequests, deferred gifts such as life insurance that will benefit your church at a later time, life-income gifts that provide lifetime income to donors and/or heirs, then be passed on, and in-kind donations.

Parish Census

Working in cooperation with the clergy and church administration, prepare a form to be used in conducting the parish census.

Distribute forms by mail or by placement in pews. Assign someone to give them out at church doors and at meetings. Distribute them in Catholic retirement homes and nursing homes, to shut-ins, and to children in parish schools for delivery to parents. As the census is compiled you will no doubt find a number of omissions, duplications, and errors. Continue to refine.

Keep census up to date. Make forms available at all times. Ask members to enter new or revised addresses, telephone numbers, or changes in family membership due to births, marriages, deaths, or because members have left the parish. See Appendix (pages 123-124) for a Census/Skills/Interest Form that is designed for computer or non-computer use. Each church task has been given a number, keyed to chapter-by-chapter assignments outlined in this book.

Personnel Policies

A church is a business as well as a spiritual center for its people. As a business organiza-

---

**ALL SAINTS PARISH
FAMILY MEMBERSHIP FORM**

Please complete one form for each individual or each family. (Include first names.)

Name: ❏ Mr.   ❏ Mrs.   ❏ Ms.
❏ Mr. and Mrs.   ❏ Miss

_____

_____

Street Address:_____

Apartment Number: _____

City: _____

State: _____

Zip Code: _____

Telephone Number:

(_____)_____

Number of Children under 15 years of age: _____

Names:

_____

_____

_____

_____

tion a church should establish personnel policies and procedures for its employees.

Prepare a Personnel Policies Manual for distribution to employees. Keep copies available in the church office.

What's to be included in the manual? First, define categories of employment such as regular full-time, regular part-time, temporary, and per-diem.

Include a statement about equal employment opportunity and sexual harassment policies, a veterans disability statement, and a policy statement about drug and alcohol abuse.

Are physical examinations or drug screenings required? If so, say so. Is a probation period necessary before appointment to the job? How about termination of employment? How is this handled?

The manual should include information on topics listed below:

• Work hours

• Holidays

• Lunch periods

• Rest breaks

• Annual leave

• Overtime

• Career development

• Dress code

• Use of telephone

• Smoking policy

What employee benefits are offered? Examples: sick leave, maternity leave, hospitalization, dental insurance, holidays, leave for jury duty (who retains jury pay?), time off for voting, retirement pensions. On what days and for what periods of time are paychecks issued?

Job Descriptions

A job description should be in place for each position, and descriptions should include at least the elements listed below:

1. Position title (Secretary, Housekeeper, Cook, Maid, Janitor, etc.).

2. Primary work functions (nutshell summary of the job).

3. Task statements (major duties and responsibilities).

4. Work Requirements:
   A. Education/knowledge (schooling/special training)
   B. Job experience
   C. Talents and abilities (skills needed to handle the job properly).

5. Appointment data:
   Who *recommends* that the person be hired
   Who *approves* the appointment
   Who *handles* the appointment
   Who *supervises* the employee

A job description for a church secretary is given on page 43.

Notary Public

A notary public is a helpful addition to the office staff of any parish.

Requirements for a notary differ from state to state and city to city but most specify that applications be approved by the town council.

Applications are submitted to the county clerk, along with a small fee. Forms will ask if applicant is a registered voter and if the applicant has been convicted of a felony, in addition to questions about address, occupation, length of residence, and education.

Applicants are asked to provide a $10,000.00 Surety Bond through an insurance company (which costs $25.00 to $50.00). The notary provides his or her own seal, obtained from an office supply firm, and must keep a record of all documents that have been signed and notarized.

Expense Reports

A variety of software systems is available to assist parishes in their bookkeeping, budgeting, and census programs. Parish Data Systems, Inc. (14425 N. 19th Avenue, Phoenix, AZ 85203; 800-999-7148) is one of many companies offering excellent programs.

Most diocesan offices will send a fiscal services representative, if requested, to assist parish accountants. In addition, parishes should have CPAs on tap to answer questions and solve problems as they arise.

The Parish and the Computer

Although the Computer Age is only twenty years old, it has become a powerful factor in our everyday lives. Most authorities agree that a parish of any size should have access to a computer console and a printer, with the services of someone who is computer literate.

As far as expense is concerned, be prepared for a sizeable budget item. However, there are individuals and corporations in every community who will make donations of money or equipment. Also, your parish should be able to find good, secondhand equipment because computer users are continually "moving up" to accommodate expanding programs.

Your parish's computer system will grow, which eventually means expenditures for expanded memory and additional software.

As for basic software, confer with your local computer experts. They probably will suggest that the parish start with these systems:

1. A word-processing program (such as WordPerfect) to write, edit, and store text.

2. A database system (such as Paradox or Power Builder) for inventories, census and membership lists, and campaign records.

3. A spreadsheet program (such as Lotus or Excel) for financial computations.

Your experts will also need to advise you about DOS vs Windows vs Macintosh, a complexity not appropriate for these pages.

Your Church as an Emergency Shelter

Most churches are in a position to render significant service by sharing their facilities in times of crisis.

Your community could be paralyzed by many types of emergencies or disasters, ranging from storm or flood to massive electrical failure. As a part of its disaster preparedness program, the American Red Cross spots potential locations where families can be sheltered. Needed are sturdy buildings in central locations with kitchen and multiple rest room facilities, large areas for sleeping, eating, and medical care. Bedding, equipment, and workers are provided by the American Red Cross.

In its efficient way, Red Cross will send specialists to meet with your people, inspect facilities and, if approved, establish contacts and contracts (including insurance protection).

ALL SAINTS PARISH
FARLEY, ILLINOIS

Job Description

POSITION TITLE:

Secretary II, Church Office

PRIMARY WORK FUNCTIONS:

This position is responsible for performing various secretarial duties under supervision of the pastor's secretary.

MAJOR JOB DUTIES AND RESPONSIBILITIES:

Types office correspondence, reports, bulletins, schedules, and newsletters.

Handles incoming and outgoing distribution of mail.

By 10 o'clock each morning, prepares first-class mailings for pick up by postman.

Prepares, or oversees preparation of, bulk rate mailings.

Maintains files and records.

Keeps supply room in order and maintains inventory levels via requisition of supplies.

Maintains record of church donations and donors. Sends notice to donors via postcard of pledge payments due.

By noon each Monday, prepares bank deposit of Saturday and Sunday church collections.

By February 1 of each year, submits to each parishioner a printed record of donations for the previous calendar year.

Answers office telephone, directs incoming calls, answers questions about Mass schedules and church services.

Answers pastor's telephone as requested.

Receives, assists, or directs visitors.

WORK REQUIREMENTS:

a. *Education and Knowledge:* graduation with secretarial training from an accredited high school; training in computer operation.

b. *Experience:* minimum of one year satisfactory secretarial experience.

c. *Skills and Abilities:* type at rate of 60 words per minute; take dictation at rate of 80 words per minute; computer literate with knowledge of WordPerfect and Lotus 1, 2, 3; knowledge of business machines; ability to plan and organize work; skill in working pleasantly and professionally with people.

APPOINTMENT DATA:

Approved by: Chairman, administration and stewardship committee

Appointed by: Pastor

Supervised by: Secretary to pastor

Chapter 3

Parish Communications

The purpose of a communications committee or team in your parish is to promote parish unity by keeping people informed about and engaged in the parish's programs and activities.

Committee Members

Potential committee members include newspaper reporters, feature writers, and editors, radio and television employees, salespersons, office workers, those in advertising, art, publicity and public relations, education, photography, magazine production. And remember the retired. Each person in your parish has a special talent that can be used.

Goals

•To promote a feeling of "belonging" among parishioners.

•To keep parish members informed about programs and activities of their church community.

•To promote the parish through church media and through community media.

•To help parish members become better informed about their faith, heritage, and Christian ethic.

•To cooperate with other committees and groups of the parish in conducting their programs.

Objectives

•*To promote a feeling of "belonging" among parishioners.*

1. Strive for a universal parish. Your church should offer activities and opportunities for every age, race, and marital status.

2. Help the parish life committee develop a newcomer packet.

3. Begin a scrapbook of newspaper articles, photographs, and mementos of parish life.

4. Sponsor a directory of parish members.

5. Develop a focus of identification, such as a parish T-shirt or bumper sticker.

•*To keep parish members informed about programs and activities of the church community.*

1. Set up an indoor bulletin board and present displays on a regular basis.

2. Publish a directory of parish groups and organizations.

3. Set up a literature rack to keep parish families informed of church programs and activities.

4. Compile a monthly calendar of parish activities.

5. Establish a telephone network to disseminate information, as needed.

6. Publish a parish newsletter. Follow bulk rate procedure in mailing it.

7. Request pulpit announcements as appropriate.

8. Support persons responsible for weekly church bulletins.

9. Provide publicity as needed for other parish committees.

• *To promote the parish through church and community media.*

1. Submit news releases and photographs about parish activities to your diocesan newsletter or to your local newspaper, radio, or TV station, or submit letters to the editor for publication in your local newspaper.

2. Suggest feature possibilities to local press, radio, or TV stations. Request editorial or cartoon.

3. Submit Mass schedules to newspapers for weekend editions. Note that many community newspapers require payment for such notices.

4. Submit basic church information to publishers of your telephone book and Yellow Pages. Include such information as name, church address and telephone number, street directions (example, "Take Main Street Exit off I-42"), Mass and confession schedules.

5. Prepare a parish visitors' guide for benefit of guests and out-of-town-visitors.

6. For a vitally important message, consider posting it on an outdoor billboard (a "24-sheeter") or on a mini-board. Some billboard companies will prepare and post such displays as a public service.

7. Prepare copy for outdoor bulletin board.

The Routine and the Bizarre

If you need to get your parish in the public eye there are scores of ways to do it, some routine, some outré. Much depends on the type of parish, the need, or the reason.

Construct a float for a holiday parade. Note that crepe paper and chicken wire have given way to scrap lumber and vinyl sheeting. The Vaughn Display Company (1700 Freeway Blvd., Minneapolis, MN 55430; 612-561-5600) offers an excellent how-to manual with its float building kits. You will need a flatbed trailer, a construction site, a squad of happy staple-gunners, and, eventually, a pull vehicle. You should be able to produce a parade float for $600 in material.

Other ways to interpret or publicize your parish: Request a newspaper editorial or a mayoral proclamation, seek time on a radio/television talk show, produce a trailer for local movie theaters, request a bench display or a bus sign.

Look for creative approaches, but conduct programs with taste and dignity. Heaven may, or may not, forgive those who resort to sound trucks and sandwich boards.

8. Share information with special organizations and groups such as religious communities, Knights of Columbus, etc.

9. Use posters, counter cards, and flyers to describe, interpret, and promote activities of the parish.

10. For major events outline and implement a complete publicity plan to be used in promoting activities and events targeted to the general community.

11. Use a release form for photographs as a matter of good business.

• *To help parish members become better informed about their faith, heritage, and Christian ethic.*

1. Support the education and formation committee in encouraging parishioners to subscribe to and read Catholic publications, including the diocesan newspaper.

2. Prepare articles about the Catholic faith, heritage, and ethic in the parish newsletter.

3. Cooperate with the education and formation committee in publicizing and promoting a parish lending library.

SPECIFIC PROJECTS IN DETAIL

Universal Parish

No doubt your parish offers programs for children, young people, and adults. Does it offer something for seniors, as well? Are parents, singles, and separated/divorced persons remembered? Does your parish offer special activities for newcomers, visitors, or foreign members?

Scrapbook

A scrapbook of newspaper clippings, posters, photographs, and mementos of parish life, available for perusal during parish get-togethers, can do much to promote a feeling of togetherness.

I suggest a newspaper-size book, available by special order through a stationer or office supply house. Use library paste or Magic Tape. (Many other brand tapes eventually become brittle.) Newspaper clippings have a tendency to crumble with time, so prepare copies on your photocopying machine. Laminate clippings if they are to be viewed by your chil-

dren's children and their children. Lamination kits are available from most office supply firms and photo finishers.

Directory of Parish Members

Many portrait studios prepare photographic directories without charge in exchange for orders received (an example: Photo Corporation of America, 815 Matthews Mint Hill Road, Matthews, NC 28105; 704-847-8011). The firms will provide help and guidance in all phases of preparation: collection of information, photo appointments, printing, promotion. The completed publications are delivered in bulk for distribution to the rejoicing recipients.

Caution: Some persons, with justification, view a church directory as an invasion of privacy. They point out that such publications can be used to obtain personal information or to build mailing lists. Be sure to discuss a directory project with your pastor and fellow church members before starting it. And be careful to respect the privacy of persons who do not want their names or personal information published.

Focus of Identification

T-shirts are now the "in" thing. Every promotion, event, and retail outlet is apt to have its own shirt. "Been there. Done that. Bought the T-shirt," is a stock phrase. But join the crowd, anyway. Young people, especially, will appreciate a special parish T-shirt or bumper sticker.

Consult Silk Screen listings in the Yellow Pages for firms producing shirts and stickers. The firms will also help with drawings and symbols. The cost of the shirt will depend on color and type of fabric. I suggest you place a minimum order, request a variety of sizes, and be prepared to reorder.

Check with parishioners about bumper stickers. Many car owners don't like them. Others seem to view their vehicles as veritable mobile billboards.

Indoor Bulletin Boards

At home the happy family gathers around the kitchen table for sharing and caring. At work everyone converges in the break room. At church the favorite focal points are often the back pews, outside steps, or the coffee pot, wherever it may be.

Try setting up a bulletin board as a new focal point. If you offer displays that are great, gripping, and grand enough, you may have a winner. And give the board a name: the Parish Exchange, Dispatch, Back Fence, Grapevine, the Main Line, the All Together, the Scoop, etc.

Change displays often. Keep your board up to the minute.

Involve amateur photographers and use lots of pictures. Encourage candid shots; never line people in rows for photographs. Eschew "grip and grin" shots of awards or presentations. For bulletin boards print your pictures large, at least 8 X 10 inches. Add a caption line naming each person, usually from left to right.

A satisfactory board can be constructed by an amateur woodworker or a high school shop class. You will need a freestanding, tripod-type board with minimum 8 X 4-foot display surface. Face the surface with cork board to receive tacks or pins. Attach a note pad and ballpoint for convenience of note takers.

Cardinal rules: easy access, easy reading. Place the board in a prominent, well-lighted area.

Vary notices. Type some. Print some. Remember that ballpoint and felt-tip pens come in many colors and widths. Use them, and remember colored paper. Add other elements to your display such as balloons, ribbons, plastic leaves and flowers, cutout letters, miniatures. Visit a hobby shop for ideas: tiny garden tools, lawn mowers, cars or trucks, miniature furniture, animals, vegetables, etc. Check with kindergarten and elementary school teachers. Most are creative in preparing bulletin board displays.

Arrange elements of your bulletin board by categories, each clearly labeled. On the following pages are examples.

BULLETINS AND BRIEFS

Note: Submit items to be posted here (notices, photographs, wants and needs, requests, day brighteners, poems, drawings, whatever) to Bob & Jean Crane, c/o Church Office, by Sunday of each week.

WHAT'S COMING UP

• Don't miss Organ Recital at 7:30 P.M. Oct 4. Miss Opal Winfred will play Bach, Widor, Dupré on sanctuary organ. Reception follows.

• Altar Server training begins Oct 14. Call Blanche White, [phone number].

• Legion of St. Mary meets in the church each Tuesday, 6:30 P.M.

• CYA picnic 2 p.m. Sept 25 at Warner Park. Call Patti at [phone number] for information.

WANTS/NEEDS

• Needed: someone to clean gutters on ranch-style house. Must supply ladder. Call [phone number].

• Mature, competent baby-sitter has Tuesdays/Thursdays free. Call Jenny Carlotti, [phone number] after 5 P.M.

• Two high school boys looking for yard work: will weed, mow, rake. Call Billy Fox, [phone number], or Andy White, [phone number].

SHARE:

• Mary Thompson's Cheese Jello was such a big hit at the open house last Thursday we asked her to share the recipe. Here it is: "two cups…"

• St. Patrick's church is seeking used furniture and appliances for a Vietnamese family. Call [phone number].

• Kitten looking for loving home. Male Siamese Seal Point. Lap kitty. Has shots. Litter trained. Call [phone number].

• Night Blooming Cereus due to bloom momentarily. Mrs. Mary Ouspenskaya wants to share the wonder. "Seeing a Cereus in bloom is almost a religious experience." Call [phone number].

• Need help on Income Tax? Barry Ogle, retired CPA, will go over your return without charge. Call [phone number].

• Marie Banks seeks passengers for day trip to Ave Maria Grotto. Share transportation expense. Call [phone number].

• The Blankenship family at Honor Farms will share okra and zucchini, a few tomatoes. Bring your own bags. Before coming call [phone number].

• Save Kroger receipts for Father Klasek at Holy Name. Only a few thousand more needed to acquire computer.

OUR TRAVELING FAMILIES:

[Photograph of Foster family at State Capitol.]

[Photograph of Bill and Ava Black on beach at Waikiki.]

[Picture post card from Delores O'Connell at Knock, Ireland.]

SALES 'N' SERVICE:

• Bill and Nancy Patterson announce a Yard Sale Saturday, June 6. There will be lots of treasure. Address: 613 Front Street.

• Kim Song has show quality Koi for sale. Call [telephone number].

NOTICES:

• Do not park in City Cafe lot. Owner needs space for customers and says he will tow violators.

• Two seats left on Oct. 25 trip to Biloxi. Call Robert Smith at [telephone number].

THE ARTISTS AMONG US:

[Post samples of watercolors from kindergarten children. Reproduce poems, drawings, paintings, etc. by parishioners.]

OUR SICK AND HOSPITALIZED: [List names of parishioners who are ill, homebound, or hospitalized.]

PRAYERS AND CANDLES: [List names of parishioners who are seriously ill or recently deceased.]

NEW FAMILIES/NEW FACES:

[List names and telephone numbers, plus photographs if available, of new parishioners.]

[Slip important papers and photographs into plastic sheet protectors while on exhibit.]

THE PAST IS PRELUDE:

[Post photographs and drawings of a historical nature. Example: early photos of church buildings, classes, interiors. For fun, include childhood photos of the clergy or some of your more prominent parishioners.]

Directory of Parish Groups and Organizations

Your parish probably includes such groups as the CYO, the DCCW, the RCIA, and the KCs, as well as the St. Vincent de Paul Society, the Altar Society, the Altar Servers, the Legion of Mary, and the Ladies of Charity. Each month will bring classes, choir rehearsals, pastoral council meetings, committee meetings, preparations for marriage and baptism. In addition, there are penance and Mass schedules. Can the parish keep up with everything?

The indoor bulletin board will help. Another aid to logic and order is a church directory. List groups alphabetically with a few words about their functions. Note meeting times and places.

Literature Rack

Metal or plastic literature racks, ranging in size from small to awesome, are available from office supply firms or stationers.

Place the rack where parishioners can browse. Work with the education and formation committee in selecting materials.

Suggestions:
Selection of Catholic publications
Literature of an inspirational nature
Parish newsletter
Current Sunday bulletin
Directory of parish groups and organizations
Monthly activities calendar
Roster of parish pastoral council members

See that the rack is checked on a regular basis and kept filled.

Monthly Calendar of Parish Activities

Each month prepare a calendar of activities. Seek input from committee chairs, function heads, and, especially, your priest and the parish secretary. Set a monthly deadline. In preparing the calendar you will need to condense, abbreviate, and consolidate.

Make notation of holidays, saint's days, schedules for Mass and the sacrament of penance. If there's room, include noteworthy birthdays and anniversaries. A golden wedding anniversary is worth noting, as is a 90th birthday, an ordination, or even a broadcast or telecast of interest.

Computer stores offer software programs for monthly calendars. A few calendars appear on the following pages.

CATHEDRAL PARISH
JANUARY 1993

S	M	T	W	T	F	S
					New Year's Day — Solemnity of Mary, Mother of God **1**	1st Saturday honors Lady Fatima Rosary after 8 AM Mass — 5:30 Sunday obligation Mass **2**
Coffee after 10 AM Mass — Epiphany of the Lord **3**	6 PM Legion of Mary meets **4**	**5**	10 AM Mass at Parthenon Towers — 7 PM Parish Council — 7:30 PM Choir **6**	**7**	**8**	5:30 Sunday obligation Mass **9**
Coffee after 10 AM Mass **10**	6 PM Legion of Mary meets **11**	**12**	7:30 PM Choir Rehearsal **13**	**14**	**15**	5:30 Sunday obligation Mass **16**
Coffee after 10 AM Mass **17**	6 PM Legion of Mary meets **18**	**19**	7:30 PM Choir Rehearsal **20**	Feast of St. Agnes **21**	Feast of St. Vincent **22**	5:30 Sunday obligation Mass **23**
Coffee after 10 AM Mass **24**	6 PM Legion of Mary meets **25**	**26**	7:30 PM Choir Rehearsal Feast of St. Angela of Merici **27**	Feast of St. Thomas Aquinas **28**	**29**	5:30 Sunday obligation Mass **30**

Masses: 7:30 AM, 10 AM, 12 PM, 6 PM (Sat. at 5:30 PM)

Cathedral of the Incarnation

2001 West End Avenue, Nashville, TN 37203

September 1987

Sacrament of Penance:
Wed: 12:45-1:30 PM
Sat: 3:30 to 5:00 PM
Other times by appointment only

Church Office: 327-2330
Cathedral "Rosary on the Air" Sun 9:15-9:30 AM
WNAH Radio (1360 am)

S	M	T	W	T	F	S
Regular Mass Schedule Sun: 7:30 AM, 10 AM, 12 PM, 6 PM Mon-Fri: 7 AM and 12:10 PM Sat: 8 AM Evening Mass at 5:30 to fulfill Sun. obl. **CCD Classes** Sun: 8:45-9:45 AM (grades 1 through high school)			10 AM Mass at Parthenon Twrs — 7:30 PM parish council — 7:30 PM choir rehearsal **1**	Feast of St. Gregory the Great — First Thursday Pray for Vocations **2**	First Friday Dedicated to the Sacred Heart — Masses at 7AM and 12:10 PM **3**	First Saturday Dedicated to Our Lady of Fatima — Rosary follows 8 AM Mass — 5:30 PM Mass of Obligation **4**	**5**
Coffee after 10 AM Mass **6**	Labor Day Parish Perpetual Rosary Day — Masses 7 AM and 12:10 PM — 6 PM Legion of Mary meets **7**	Feast of birthday of the blessed Mother **8**	Feast of St. Peter Claver **9**	7:30 PM choir rehearsal **10**	**11**	Marian Year Rosary follows 8 AM Mass — 5:30 PM Mass of Obligation **12**
Coffee after 10 AM Mass and before noon Mass — 7 PM CYO meets **13**	Feast of the Triumph of the Cross — 6 PM Legion of Mary meets **14**	Feast of Our Lady of Sorrows **15**	Feast of Sts. Cornelius and Cyprian, martyrs **16**	Feast of St. Robert Bellarmine — 7:30 PM choir rehearsal **17**	**18**	Marian Year Rosary follows 8 AM Mass — Feast of St. Januarius — 5:30 PM Mass **19**
Coffee after 10 AM Mass — CCD Registration after Masses — Parish picnic 1:15 Hachland Hill **20**	Feast of St. Matthew — 6 PM Legion of Mary meets — 7 PM ecumenical prayer service and reception **21**	7 PM Rededication Mass in Cathedral — Reception follows in courtyard **22**	**23**	7:00 PM RCIA classes begin in St. Albert Hall **24**	**25**	Feast of Sts. Cosmos and Damien — Marian Year Rosary follows 8 AM Mass — 5:30 PM Mass **26**
Coffee after 10 AM Mass — Special guest: Sr. Gerarda from our adopted parish in Haiti **27**	1 PM Cathedral DCCW meets in St. Albert Hall — 6 PM Legion of Mary meets in rectory **28**	Feast of Sts. Michael, Gabriel, and Raphael, archangels **29**	Feast of St. Jerome 7:30 choir rehearsal **30**	**Date to remember:** "Living Rosary" October 4th at 3 PM in Cathedral, followed by reception in St. Albert Hall		

Telephone Network

A telephone network is the least inexpensive and most efficient means of spreading information. Success depends on an advance organization of dependable participants.

If twenty persons each agree to call four persons, and each of these four agree to call four more, a total 320 families or individuals will be reached in short order.

A suggested call sheet is reproduced here:

Attention: <u>Mrs. Belle O'Phone</u>
     2222 Apple Valley Drive
     Alexandria, TX 37205
     (Telephone 555-0040)

Thank you for agreeing to be a part of our Telephone Network. Because of this program important information can be distributed quickly to members of our parish.

Our pastor reports that there has been a poor response so far to next month's Heritage Dinner and has asked our Telephone Network to help promote it. Therefore, we ask that you place telephone calls to these four persons or families:

     1. Adam Thomas, Jr., Tel 555-3340
     2. Mr. and Mrs. J. J. Walker, Tel 555-2220
     3. Robert and Betty Bowen, Tel 555-9958
     4. Anise Black, Tel 555-3307

Encourage them to attend our Heritage Dinner at 7 P.M. Tuesday, February 3. They should make reservations by calling Mary in the church office, telephone number 555-3999. Ask everyone to bring a covered dish. Parishioners are encouraged to wear native costumes reflecting their heritage and culture. There will be folk dancing and special entertainment.

Ask each person to place a telephone call to four additional families (of their choosing) to spread word of the Heritage Dinner.

Make contact as soon as possible so your families will have time to place their calls... and thank you again for being a part of our Telephone Network.

Parish Newsletter

Very few programs can exceed the parish newsletter as a source of communication, inspiration, and motivation. Publish your newsletter at least four times a year.

Include such features as a letter from the pastor, profiles of parish members, articles and photographs about parish activities and organizations, articles of a historical nature, book reviews, recipes, poetry, humor, sections for both seniors and youth, articles offering help or guidance, thoughts on inspiration, faith, and prayer. Also, include articles of a more secular nature such as preparation of Christian wills, control of stress, importance of blood pressure checks, accident prevention, home and highway safety.

Before you put together your first issue, decide the tone that you want to convey. Some publications take the "newsletter" approach using newspaper style and format for the busy reader. Others reach for something more permanent, featuring articles that can be read now or a year from now, publications that can be kept on family bookshelves with other Christian literature. Choose, but be consistent.

The committee preparing the newsletter should include artists as well as writers, persons who are computer literate, and someone knowledgeable about printing and mailing.

For illustrations and artwork, many clip art

Follow Bulk Rate/Third Class Procedures in Mailing Newsletter

Does your church mailing list include at least 200 names? If so you can save money by sending your newsletter (and other mailing pieces) bulk rate.

The U.S. post office offers a special rate for church mailings. Certain conditions must be met in order to qualify. Meet with a postal representative to determine what these requirements are.

Bulk or third-class rates are not available to individuals; only organizations and churches are eligible for a special rate in the third-class category.

Requirements and procedures change continually, but here is an overview of what's in place at this writing.

First requirement: pay approximately $150 in post office fees.

Half of this is an annual fee; the other half covers cost of a bulk mail permit. A number of forms must be completed, but questions are easy, and any church will have access to the necessary documents.

If your church qualifies for bulk mailing, the post office will issue a permit number to be printed on the newsletter with other information such as "US POSTAGE PAID, BULK RATE, NON-PROFIT ORGANIZATION." This indicia, as it is called, is placed in a small square on the face of the mailing piece.

Preparation of your first bulk rate mailing can be tedious, but learn the procedures and your second mailing will be easier.

Third-class mailings require at least 200 pieces (identical).

The mailing must be separated into the following categories:

1. Five-digit groups (Example, all addressed to zip code 37203)

2. Three-digit groups (Example, all addressed to zip codes beginning 372__) to addresses within one state

3. Addresses in mixed states

The process involves patience, careful count, a host of rubber bands, gummed labels, and grimy mail sacks as provided by the post office.

Mailing pieces must not be too small or too large. "Just right," according to post office regulations is at least 3½ inches high and at least 5 inches long—but not more than 11¾ inches in width or 14 inches in length. A standard letter-size sheet, folded, is O.K. Affix pages in some fashion. Stapling is allowed, but staples are apt to break fingernails. Paper sealers, as found in office supply stores, make mailings easier to open.

programs are available in software stores, and a number of mail order firms offer liturgical art service. Two such firms are Tarrywood Design Inc. (P.O. Box 81, Bristol, CT 06011-00810) and the Fellowship of Merry Christians, Inc. (P.O. Box 895, Portage, MI 49081-099;1-800-877-2757). Liguori Publications in Liguori, Missouri, and The Liturgical Press in Collegeville, Minnesota, supply art images and fillers on disk. Prices are reasonable for an outpouring of art and ideas.

Sunday Bulletins

Sunday bulletin covers are available from the Liturgical Press or Liguori Publications. Inside pages are left blank for parish use. Prices range from $2.50 to $3.50 per hundred, plus shipping. Liguori also offers a Spanish/English format.

A number of parishes sell advertising space in their bulletins or newsletters. Some solicit their own advertisers. Others find it more advantageous to engage a service company such as Liturgical Publications (headquartered in St. Louis, MO) to handle the sale of advertisements.

News Releases

Submit news releases to local newspapers and to local radio and television stations. Place a telephone call first to be sure your material can be used. Ask if editors prefer mail or FAX. If FAX, ask for the FAX number.

FAXes

Don't let a FAX faze you. The term is short for *facsimile,* a process of sending printed material by telephone. FAX machines are now found in nearly every radio and newspaper office, most businesses, and many churches.

Before you send a message it is wise to call the receiver's telephone number to say a FAX is coming. Someone can then check to see that the machine is turned on and that your message is received.

You will find the machine easy to operate. Approach it with confidence. Enter the FAX number, then feed in your first sheet (most times upside down). When the line is answered, punch "Send." After transmission, the FAX machine will spit back your original copy, usually with a note of date and time transmitted. Keep this for your records.

Difficulty in FAXing could mean, (1) the receiver's line is busy, (2) the receiving machine is not turned on, (3) your outgoing message has been blocked by an incoming FAX message, (4) you entered a telephone number rather than a FAX number, or maybe, (5) you dialed wrong. Try again.

On the next page is a pattern for a news release.

Postage Meter

If your cost of postage ranges from $50 to $76 a month, consider renting a postage meter. Advantages: indicia records the mailing date, city, amount of postage. Meters eliminate stamps, dispense exact postage, simplify bulk mailings, speed postal delivery. Also, they feature personalized messages which, according to the meter people, have "high exposure."

The meter message, which can consist of up to 28 characters, is printed by means of a special "ad plate." Many churches have seasonal messages that they reuse every year. Plates also can display photographs, say of the church or altar. Color is available. Meters are rented from independent mailing machine companies. Call one of them to determine if a postage meter would benefit your church.

Release to: THE DAILY HERALD
222 Main Street
Townsville, TN 37204
FAX # 555-8822

From: Mary Smith, All Saints Church
Telephone 555-4498

At least 200 children's books and toys have been requested by the Holy Rosary Catholic Church for children at the Bleakbrook Orphanage.

According to Mary Smith, projects coordinator, the items should be clean, in good working order, and appropriate for six- to ten-year-olds. The drive is part of Holy Rosary's program for homeless children. Last year residents of orphanages across the state were given clothing, linens, and special food.

"Some of the children at Bleakbrook have never had a toy they could call their own," Ms. Smith said. "Our goal is to provide at least three toys and two books for each child in the orphanage." For younger children she requested blocks, pull toys, or coloring books; for older children, balls and bats, kites, games, and books suitable for beginning readers.

Toys and other items should be brought to the church's educational building, 439 Meadow Lane, between 2 and 6 P.M. Monday through Friday.

Those wishing additional information should call Ms. Smith at 555-4498.

#   #   #

A sample news release. See pages 55-56.

No handwritten notes. You can find a typewriter. Use it to prepare the release, and save a copy for your files.

Note that the name, mailing address, and FAX number of the newspaper is placed at the top. Next, place your name and telephone number or name of person to be called if additional information is needed.

Enter at least six lines of space before beginning your release so the editor of the publication can scribble in a headline or instruction to his printer. Most editors prefer to enter their own headlines, so don't title your article.

Now, forget all laws of logic and beauty by cramming everything into the first sentence. This means everything, especially the "5 Ws

and the H" of the newspaper world: who, what, when, where, why, and how. Note that the release reproduced here tells *who* is involved, *what* is needed and *why*, *where* items go, and *when* they are needed. In addition, the reader is told *how* to obtain additional information.

At the close of the release, insert a symbol such as " # # # " or "end" to indicate that's all there is. If copy runs longer than one page (bad idea), number the pages at top right, "1 of 2," "2 of 2," etc.

O.K., you have prepared your releases and are ready to mail, FAX, or hand deliver them.

You now need a media list (names, addresses, telephone and FAX numbers of newspapers, radio and television stations). Lists can be obtained from your Chamber of Commerce, from state press and broadcast associations, or borrowed from a cooperative public relations person.

You can compile your own list from the Yellow Pages (consult listings under Newspapers, Radio Stations, Television Stations), but you will need to call each listing for the mailing address or FAX number. A benefit from such calls, however, is that you can find out exactly when and to whom material should be sent. Your contact person will depend on the size and structure of the newspaper. It might be the city editor, a religious editor if the paper has one, the state desk, or (sometimes) the society editor. Obtain specific names and titles for best results.

If you plan extensive contacts with the media you may consider a professional directory, which can cost from $80 to $1,000. An excellent but inexpensive one is the *All-In-One Media Directory,* which can be ordered from the Gebbie Press, Box 1000, New Paltz, NY 12601.

Radio and TV Newsrooms

Make contact with radio or TV newsrooms only if your material is Big News. You probably could attract mike & camera people to a giant ground breaking, a really big new program, or a well-known visiting VIP, but most parish events are considerably less newsworthy.

During holiday periods news departments often cover Masses, colorful ceremonies, or soup kitchen activities. If you are friends with radio or television newspeople, ask them to check your parish on their "slow" days. You, in turn, should keep in mind some of those activities that are worth covering.

Your parish can sponsor a program of rosaries on the air. Most radio stations offer special church rates, varying from $85 to $100 per month, for which your priest can record a 45-

minute series of 15-minute rosaries. Selections from this series are broadcast each Sunday morning throughout the year.

Public Service Director

A special approach is needed for parish announcements and appeals. In most instances this material is taken, not to the radio/TV news department, but to the public service director, who will schedule it without charge. If we paid for public service air time, incidentally, we'd be speaking of hundreds, often thousands of dollars.

Don't make demands on your radio or TV station because you think the law requires them to give time to churches and welfare agencies. They are required to schedule a certain amount of public service time, yes, but such time could include weather information and news reports.

Include a cover letter with material you submit. Explain who you are, the nature of your announcement, and why you need air time.

In preparing material to be submitted list the name of the radio or TV station at top left, followed by your name and telephone number (or the name of the person to be called for additional information). Also, indicate the date you want the announcement to start and the date you want it to stop.

Note that words in a public service announcement or "PSA" are counted and an indication is given of the time needed to read them. Announcers speak at various speeds but, generally, 20 to 25 words can be read in ten seconds, 25-30 words require fifteen seconds, 30-35 words require twenty seconds, and 40-50 words can be read in 30 seconds.

A suggested cover letter and sample PSAs are outlined on the following pages.

ST. MARY CHURCH

444 Main Street, N.W.
Harvey, Texas 22229

Memo to: Public Service Directors
           Radio Stations

Re: Fun Fest and Craft Fair

We enclose a sheet of PSAs concerning our third annual Fun Fest and Craft Fair, which is scheduled for August 21.

The affair provides much needed financial support for our St. Mary charities, including such programs as the Room in the Inn emergency shelter, the "Loaves & Fishes" family food program, the Matthew XXV assist for troubled persons, and the "Reading is Fundamental" literacy program for adults. Charities also include the day-by-day feeding and disbursing of assistance to stranded, destitute, or burned-out families.

We hope you can help in publicizing the event. I will be happy to arrange interviews at any time. If you wish additional information please call me at 555-4444.

Thank you.

Virginia Steele
Publicity Chairman
Fun Fest and Craft Fair
St. Mary Church
Encl.

Sample public service cover letter. See page 57.

Release to: Public Service Directors

From: Virginia Steel, 555-4444

Please schedule July 31 through August 21. Kill August 21.

10-Second Spot Announcement (30 Words)

Visit the Fun Fest and Craft Fair on Saturday, August 21, at St. Mary's Catholic Church, 444 West Main Street. Hours: from 10:00 A.M. until 4:00 P.M. Admission is free.

20-Second Spot Announcement (55 Words)

Harvey's St. Mary Church will hold its third annual Fun Fest and Craft Fair from 10:00 A.M. to 4:00 P.M. on Saturday, August 21. There will be food and entertainment, a bake sale, a flea market, an arts and crafts sale, carnival games, and a children's corner. Everyone is invited. There is no charge for admission, and free parking is available.

30-Second Announcement (90 Words)

The third annual Fun Fest and Craft Fair is scheduled Saturday, August 21, on the grounds of St. Mary's Church, 444 West Main Street. Church officials expect more than a thousand friends and families to attend. Proceeds will go to St. Mary's charities.

The event will feature food, music and entertainment, arts and crafts, carnival games, a children's corner, a bake sale, and flea market buys.

Hours will be from 10:00 A.M. to 4:00 P.M. The public is invited. There is no admission charge, and free parking will be available.

# # #

Sample public service announcement. See page 57.

Release to: Radio WPXI
From: Todd Parkes, Tel 555-0040

PUBLIC SERVICE ANNOUNCEMENT
Please schedule Monday, April 2, through Saturday, April 7. Kill April 7.

20-Second Announcement (55 words)

A Health Fair is scheduled from 9:00 A.M. to 9:00 P.M.. Saturday at St. Mary Catholic Church on Main Street. Registered nurses will be on hand to offer screening for blood pressure, hearing, and vision. The tests are free and open to the public. For more information call Todd Parkes at the church, 555-0040.

15-Second Announcement (25 words)

A Health Fair is scheduled this Saturday at St. Mary Catholic Church on Main Street. Free tests will be offered for blood pressure, hearing, and vision. For full information call 555-0040.

10-Second Announcement (20 words)

A Health Fair is scheduled this Saturday at St. Mary Church on Main Street. For full information call Todd Parkes at 555-0040.

Sample public service announcement. See page 57.

Mass Schedules in Newspapers, Telephone Books, and Yellow Pages

Many newspapers require payment for Mass notices. Call to find out. If you decide on a paid schedule each Sunday, you will need to include the cost in your annual budget. The notice should include the name, address, and telephone number of your church in addition to the Mass schedule, days and times for the sacrament of penance, etc. Boxed notices are pricey but more visible.

Include similar information for listings in the telephone book or the Yellow Pages. For the benefit of out-of-town visitors, include street directions such as "Take Main Street Exit off Highway 42."

Parish Visitors' Guide

Your church probably is visited by more people than you ever imagined: individuals and families from other parishes or other states, perhaps other countries. Some are Catholic, some Protestant, and some unchurched. A guide to your church and parish could be of great benefit.

It can be as simple or elaborate as you wish, from a single sheet to a many splendored, full-sized publication. Include a brief history of the parish and offer a self-guided tour of the building.

Who founded the church? When? Where did the altar or the baptismal font come from? What do the windows represent? Has the building been the scene of any significant events?

Outdoor Bulletin Board

Prepare copy to be posted on an outdoor bulletin board. Include Mass information, announcement of special meetings, speakers, plus epigrams and one-liners.

For one-liners and epigrams consult *14,000 Quips and Quotes* by E.C. McKenzie, *The Speaker's Quote Book* and *Uncle Ben's Instant Quote Book* by Benjamin R. De Jong. The three books are published by Baker Book House.

Memos to Special Organizations and Groups

When your parish plans a major event, share information with special organizations and groups such as religious communities, Knights of Columbus, the DCCW, the CYO, senior citizen centers, retirement complexes and nursing homes, clubs, and councils of the diocese.

Below is a sample memo promoting a Fun Fest and Craft Fair that was addressed to the Knights of Columbus.

MEMO

TO: Knights of Columbus
From: Virginia Steele, Craft Fair Chairman
Re: August Craft Fair

The third annual Craft Fair, sponsored by the parish council of St. Mary Church, is scheduled for Saturday, August 21, from 10:00 A.M. to 4:00 P.M. More than a thousand families and friends of the church are expected.

We hope members of such diocesan organizations as the Knights of Columbus will support the Craft Fair, as well. Enclosed is a poster for your bulletin board. Also, we request that you make an announcement to your membership.

There will be food, music and entertainment, carnival games, a children's corner, a book and flea market, arts and crafts, a bake sale, and a theater presentation of magic. St. Mary Church charities are to receive all proceeds from the day's events.

There is no charge for admission and everybody is invited. If you have questions or suggestions please call us at 555-0040. Thank you.
Encl.

Posters, Counter Cards, and Flyers

To promote activities and programs use posters, leaflets, and counter cards (cards printed both sides and folded, tent-like, for counter tops). Use colored paper to best catch attention. On the facing page is a sample poster that was generated by computer.

Publicity Plan

You will seldom need such an elaborate plan, but for a *big* event requiring major promotion, here is the framework. Begin at least six months in advance. Determine media targets (general public, the unchurched, young adults, parents, Catholics only, etc.), map out releases, set up deadlines.

Publicity Plan for an Event Scheduled for August 21

Week of May 17
- Make appointments for August radio and TV interviews.

Week of June 7
- Finalize mailing lists and prepare labels (radio/TV stations, newspapers, shopping guides, merchants with outdoor marquee signs, malls, other churches, senior homes, religious communities, KC councils, college publications, and radio stations).
- Prepare article for parish newsletter.

Week of June 14
- Finalize news releases, radio public service announcements, letters, flyers, posters.

Week of June 21
- Reproduce releases, letters, etc. for distribution
- Prepare for mailing (affix labels, stuff envelopes). (FAXing will begin July 26.)

- Mail memos to churches within diocese.
- Mail information to in-house publications and personnel directors of business, industry, PR firms.

Week of June 28
- Request mention from your pulpit and in bulletin on Sunday, July 4.

Week of July 5
- Place print order for posters, flyers (July 26 delivery).
- Place orders for T-shirts, banners, balloons, bumper stickers, buttons, etc. (July 26 delivery).
- Make contact with daily newspapers to request feature articles, photographs.

Week of July 12
- Recruit volunteers to deliver posters, flyers to neighborhood merchants, restaurants, fast-food outlets, beauty and barber shops, garages and service stations, schools, civic and community buildings, etc.
- Mail letters to merchants requesting messages on outdoor marquees.

Week of July 19
- Request mention from your pulpit and in bulletin on Sunday, July 25.

(continued on page 64)

Cathedral of the Incarnation

Fun Fest &
Craft Fair

Saturday
Aug 21
10 am to
4 pm

Bake Sale
Flea Market
Games/Crafts
Food/Drinks
Entertainment

Week of July 26

- Volunteers distribute posters to neighborhood merchants and other locations as listed above (week of July 12).
- Mail or FAX releases to weekly newspapers, shopping center and mall publications, shopper guides, college media.
- Mail material to senior centers, retirement homes, religious communities, KC councils.
- Have T-shirts, balloons, buttons, bumper stickers been received?

Week of August 2

- Mail/FAX releases to radio public service directors.
- Put up outdoor banners.
- Request mention from your pulpit and in bulletin for Sunday, August 8.
- Make telephone calls to follow through on releases submitted to date. "Did you receive my material? Will you be able to use it? Need more information?"
- Begin sale of T-shirts, distribution of balloons, buttons, and bumper stickers.

Week of August 9

- Have neighborhood shopping centers and malls been called to request information tables? If not, get in touch with them.
- Mail or FAX releases to daily newspapers. Follow through with telephone calls.
- Request mention from your pulpit and in bulletin for Sunday, August 15.
- Prepare parish flyers or brochures for distribution on Sunday, August 15.

Week of August 16

- Arrange for note of appreciation to appear in bulletin on Sunday, August 22. Request a verbal thank-you from the pulpit. Prepare letters of appreciation for supporters and workers.

Photo Releases

Always obtain permission from authorities before taking photographs in hospitals, nursing homes, retirement centers, shelters, meal sites, or places of refuge. For reasons of pride and privacy, do not photograph people who are receiving service. Generally speaking, a photo release is never out of line, even though subjects agree verbally. The pattern can be simple.

> I give permission to (name of parish)_____ to use my photograph and pertinent information in its newsletter.
>
> (Signature) _____
>
> (Address) _____
>
> (City, State, Zip) _____
>
> (Telephone Number) _____ (Date) _____

After obtaining signatures, place the release in a file folder with negatives and notation of when/where the photograph was taken and when/where it appeared.

Chapter 4

Education and Formation

The purpose of an education and formation committee or team in your parish is to plan and coordinate the parish's educational mission.

Committee Members

The education and formation committee should be made up of persons with training, knowledge, or interest in religious education: teachers, librarians, nursery and day care workers. Include those involved in the parish's religious education program and youth ministry. If your parish has a parochial school, include the principal or a liaison from the school board.

Goals

• To coordinate a policy of religious education for the parish.

• To promote religious education in the parish.

Objectives

• *To coordinate a policy of religious education for the parish.*

1. Make parishioners aware of the catechetical mission of the church.

2. Assist in linking catechetical, liturgical, and service ministries.

• *To promote religious education in the parish.*

1. Support the school board committee.

2. Assist the religious education director in presenting a strong program.

3. Assist pastor in implementing a program of sacramental preparation and catechesis for the parish.

4. Assist religious education director in presenting religious education classes for children in public schools.

5. Assist RCIA director and religious education director in preparing and presenting the Rite of Christian Initiation for Adults (RCIA).

   A. Prepare an RCIA newsletter that will report on catechetical progress of participants, give recognition to teachers and workers, and publicize first communion and confirmation ceremonies.

   B. Coordinate receptions following RCIA ceremonies.

6. Coordinate the children's first communion and confirmation.

7. Sponsor classes/training in such subjects as the catechism, Bible study, church history, sacraments, and ceremonies.

8. Assume responsibility for establishment or maintenance of church nursery and encourage

use of the nursery during Masses.

9. Encourage subscriptions to Catholic publications.

10. Establish and maintain a parish lending library or bookshelf.

A. Recruit a librarian to develop and implement plans and budgeting for a parish lending library or bookshelf.

B. Identify volunteers to carry out the program.

C. Work with the communications committee in preparing and distributing flyers promoting the library.

D. Develop and implement a children's program in the library.

SPECIFIC PROJECTS IN DETAIL

Religious Education

Religious education is a major concern of the entire parish.

The education and formation committee supports the school board committee and cooperates with it in its service to parochial schools.

For those not in parochial schools, the education and formation committee supports adult education and religious education programs.

Religious education programs vary from parish to parish. The one described here was developed by Mary Mac Boyd, religious education director for the Cathedral of the Incarnation in Nashville.

Mrs. Boyd is assisted by twenty-two volunteer teachers who were recruited from the church community. After joining the group, they attended orientation and in-service training. In addition, they were given an explanation and demonstration of resources and equipment.

The religious education program is arranged in four sections:

1. Pre School: 3-year-olds through kindergarten. Classes meet during 10 o'clock Mass.

(Text: "I Am Special" from Our Sunday Visitor)

2. Elementary: first through sixth grade. Classes meet from 8:45 to 9:45 on Sunday mornings.

(Text: the "Focus" Series from Brown-ROA)

Grade 1: Loving (God, our loving creator)

Grade 2: Belonging (baptism, reconciliation, eucharist)

Grade 3: Believing (Creed offers guide to show church as community of loving friends)

Grade 4: Living (Christian morality)

Grade 5: Celebrating (Liturgical life, prayer, sacraments)

Grade 6: Relating (Old and New Testaments, showing how church people through the years have related to God and vice versa)

3. Preparatory (Grades 7-8): Classes meet from 4:45 to 5:45 on Sunday afternoons.

Grade 7: Personal growth, relationships, human sexuality

Grade 8: Confirmation. Candidates attend a retreat as part of their confirmation preparation. Students select service projects such as aid to the elderly, help in the nursery, assistance to the homeless.

(Text for Grades 7 and 8: the "Connects" series from Silver, Burdett, Ginn.)

4. *High School* (Grades 9-12):

Grade 9: Students use a liturgy-based catechism

Grade 10-12: Students use lectionary-based readings and discussions.

In addition to these classes, the program provides training in sacramental preparation:

the eucharist

reconciliation

confirmation

Additional text: "Spirit Magazine" offers weekly ideas and suggestions for teachers.

Equipment for the religious education program: In addition to telephone facilities, this includes TV and VCR units, an audiocassette player, slide and filmstrip projectors, and access to a photocopy machine and computer.

Reproduced below and on the following pages are sample promotional flyers and a registration form for a religious education program.

Sample promotional flyer

ALL SAINTS CHURCH
N O T I C E !

Sunday School Classes

3- and 4-year olds and kindergarten
First — Sixth Grade
Seventh—Twelfth Grade
Begin Sunday, September 11

Classes for 3- and 4-year-olds and kindergarten will meet during 10:00 Mass on Sunday Morning in the first floor of the education building.

Classes for grades one through six will meet from 8:45 until 9:45 on Sunday morning on the 3rd floor of our education building

Classes for grades seven through twelve will meet on Sunday afternoons from 4:45 until 5:45 on the 2nd floor of our education building.

If your student was not preregistered, please complete the form on the back of this sheet and drop it in the collection, or bring it with you on the first day of class.

ALL SAINTS CHURCH CREDO PREP PROGRAM

Registration Form

NAME: _____

ADDRESS: _____

TELEPHONE NUMBER: _____BIRTHDAY: _____

FATHER'S NAME: _____

    RELIGION: _____

    OCCUPATION: _____

MOTHER'S NAME: _____

    RELIGION: _____

    OCCUPATION: _____

BAPTISM DATE: _____

    NAME OF CHURCH: _____

    ADDRESS OF CHURCH: _____

FIRST EUCHARIST: _____

    NAME OF CHURCH: _____

    ADDRESS OF CHURCH: _____

CONFIRMATION DATE: _____

    NAME OF CHURCH: _____

    ADDRESS OF CHURCH: _____

NAME: _____

SCHOOL: _____ GRADE: _____

Sample promotional announcement

ALL SAINTS PARISH
MINISTRY TO CHILDREN

ALL SAINTS CHURCH OFFERS THESE CLASSES FOR CHILDREN:

• Infants to 18 months: Nursery on Sundays during 10:00 o'clock Mass

• 19 months to three years: Toddler Nursery on Sundays during 10 o'clock Mass

• Three- to five-year-olds: class on Sundays during 10:00 o'clock Mass

• First through sixth grade: class on Sundays 8:45 A.M. to 9:45 A.M.

• Seventh grade through high school: class on Sundays 4:45 P.M. to 5:45 P.M.

• Six- to ten year-year-olds are invited to take part in the children's liturgy of the word during 10:00 o'clock Mass each Sunday. This is not a class but a celebration of the liturgy of the word that has been especially designed for children.

For additional information about classes call the Religious Education Director at the church office, 555-5555.

For information about the children's liturgy call Esther Cook, 555-4545.

Rite of Christian Initiation for Adults (RCIA)

Members of the education and formation committee should know and understand the RCIA process in order to lend assistance and support as it is needed.

The program is conducted by the RCIA director, who is appointed by the pastor. With support of the director of religious education, the RCIA director is assisted by approximately ten team members.

Members of the education and formation committee can serve on the RCIA team or assist in recruiting members of the team. They can assist the RCIA director in planning and presenting programs and in recruiting sponsors and catechists.

Catechumens (persons who have not been baptized) and candidates (baptized, but uncatechized persons seeking full communion with the church [confirmation, eucharist]) are paired with sponsors for the course of the program.

The RCIA has four stages: (1) Inquiry, (2) Catechumenate, (3) Purification/Enlightenment, and (4) Mystagogy.

A workable formula for RCIA sessions: prayer, presentation of subject by catechist, a general discussion followed by a break into small groups for personal application, reconvening for final questions, and a closing prayer.

1. During the Inquiry stage, persons learn about the faith, reach the point of initial conversion, and express a desire to become Christians. Basic information is presented about the Catholic Church and how it differs from other churches. Beliefs in God and Jesus, Mary, and

the Saints are brought into the discussion, as well as prayerful exploration of the Bible. The stage concludes with "the Rite of Acceptance into the Order of Catechumens."

2. During the Catechumenate stage, the catechumens receive pastoral formation and guidance to help them become disciples. Catechesis during this time includes dogmas and precepts and a keen awareness of the mystery of salvation. Celebrations of the Word are at the heart of the catechumenate.

3. When the catechumens are ready—and the church agrees that they are ready—then they enter the period of Purification and Enlightenment, a time of more intense, final preparation for the sacraments of initiation. The period usually coincides with the season of Lent and begins with the Rite of Election, usually celebrated on the First Sunday of Lent, when these catechumens have their names enrolled in the Book of the Elect. For these new elect, this is a time for reflection, along with the entire church, a time to resolve final questions.

On the third, fourth, and fifth Sundays of Lent, the elect take part in "the Rites of Scrutiny" which, again, are moments of introspection and evaluation.

The sacraments of initiation—baptism, confirmation, eucharist—are celebrated, normally at the Easter Vigil.

4. The fourth and final step in RCIA is Mystagogy, when the newly baptized—now called neophytes—are given support and assistance in taking their place as active disciples in the church community.

The RCIA team helps with Inquiry (contacts speakers, checks attendance, assists in conducting programs). It helps those in charge of sponsors (to train, guide, and oversee), and those who handle music, promotion, and publicity, as well as the all-important matter of refreshments.

Classes/Training

To learn is to find fulfillment, to grow and expand, to share, and to come together as a group. Cooperate with the clergy in selecting topics, selecting speakers, and scheduling classes.

The Church Nursery

An important responsibility of the education and formation committee is the establishment and maintenance of a church nursery.

A. If there is a need, establish two nurseries: a baby nursery for infants up to 18 months, and a toddler nursery for those 19 months to three years of age.

B. Use imagination in decorating. The entry door gives the first impression, so make it inviting. Paint chairs and tables in bright colors (non-toxic paint!). Apply patterns to the ceiling. Consider a play-game carpet (many patterns are available at floor and hardware stores). Frame biblical posters for the walls or install corkboard panels and decorate with balloons, drawings, and pictures. For this, use staples, adhesive tape, string, or glue instead of tacks and pins that could end up in small mouths. Provide coatracks at heights suitable for the children.

C. Inspect the nursery for needs, shortcomings. Obtain equipment or materials as necessary.

Keep the following criteria in mind:

1. The area should be clean, maintained at a comfortable temperature, and have an adequate staff of trained aides. The toy box should be stocked with safety-approved toys. Cast aside anything with sharp edges, lead

paint, or detachable parts that could be swallowed. Place child's safety plugs on all electrical receptacles. If there is an outside play area, fence it and see that grass, sand, or wood chips are placed where children might fall.

2. Nursery supplies should include books/coloring tablets.

3. Emergency medical assistance should be available. Your parish membership no doubt includes nurses, pediatricians, or general practitioners. Ask one to be on call.

4. A quiet area should be set aside with pallets and clean blankets so guests can nap if they grow tired.

5. Cleaners, insecticides, matches, paints, varnishes, or other potentially hazardous materials should be kept under lock and key, and situated *far* from the nursery.

D. Publicize the nursery via posters, bulletin notices, word of mouth. Request announcements from the pulpit. Prepare an article for the church newsletter. Ask ushers to mention the nursery to parents of small children. Search for attention-getting ways of promoting the nursery, such as messages on paper toys, tote bags, pink and blue balloons.

E. Work with the communications committee in preparing a flyer promoting the nursery for placement in pews. Suggestions for such a flyer are given below:

Flyer Promoting the Church Nursery

In preparing a flyer to promote the church nursery, emphasize features that would appeal to parents, such as:

Convenient, nearby location

Safe place for children

Comfortable environment (heated/air cooled)

St. Mary's Sunday Nursery

Announcing the opening of our parish's Sunday nursery (available during the 10 AM and noon Masses).

- Staffed by trained aides
- Safe, supervised, and clean
- Infants to age five welcome
- Mother-approved
- Tender, loving care
- Safe toys and equipment

We will baby your baby while you attend Mass.

Parents invited to visit!

Announcing the

PARISH NURSERY

Safe, convenient child care provided for children ages one to four during 10 AM and noon Masses.

- Our supervisor is an experienced day care provider.

- A nurse is on call.

- Our staff has had intensive training and extensive experience.

- The nursery has just been remodeled with fresh paint and bright, cheerful lighting.

- The equipment and toys are safety checked and approved.

- The nap area is warm and quiet.

- Crayons and coloring books are provided.

Modern fixtures, well lighted
Play area inspected for hazards
Quiet, clean nap area
Safe toys and equipment
Careful selection of books, coloring books
Experienced supervisor, trained aides
Nurse on call
Individual attention to each child
Tender loving care (TLC)
Happy atmosphere
Infant Nursery designed for Infants to age 18 months
Toddler Nursery for children 19 months to three years
Mother-approved

Reproduce your flyer on pink or blue paper.

Lending Library

A modest expenditure of time and money will go far in promoting the presence of Christian literature in homes of your parish.

You will need at least $1,000 to begin a family bookshelf or lending library. This includes an initial expenditure of about $500, plus from $25 to $50 each month for new purchases.

Solicit books from parishioners. Encourage memorial gifts. Request discounts from suppliers and bookstores.

Include in your inventory such volumes as:
Catechism of the Catholic Church
The New American Bible
The New American Bible, Giant Print Edition
The Catholic Study Bible (Oxford)
Bible commentary
Bible dictionary
"The Sunday Liturgy of the Word and Catechetical Planning Guide" (Treehaus)
The Lectionary for Masses with Children (USCC)

The Official Catholic Directory
The Catholic Almanac
The Catholic Source Book (Brown-ROA)
A diocesan directory
A Catholic dictionary
A general dictionary
A Catholic encyclopedia
A general encyclopedia
Church calendar
A concordance
Plus, of course, *The Parish Activities Handbook*

Include video programs, audio tapes/books
in such categories as:
  Bible study
  Books for children and young people
  Church history
  Contemporary problems
  Doctrine
  Evangelization
  Lay ministry
  Lives of the saints
  Marriage
  Prayer and devotions

Subscriptions to Catholic Publications

Catholics have a wealth of publications at their disposal. Sadly, many parishioners seldom read them. Here are some to consider:

NEWSPAPERS
Your diocese probably has its own newspaper. Some publish foreign language editions if a good proportion of their subscribers cannot read English.

Our Sunday Visitor, the largest English-print Catholic publication in the world, is a weekly tabloid in newspaper format, printed in black and white and color. Contents include news, features, and columns.

The Twin Circle, a weekly tabloid type newspaper, printed in black and white and color. Includes news, features, and columns of general interest.

The National Catholic Register, a full-sized newspaper published weekly, printed in black and white, is the granddaddy of the diocesan newspapers. No features or columns but news of special interest to the Catholic community.

The National Catholic Reporter, a black and white weekly tabloid type newspaper including news and feature articles.

MAGAZINES
Catholic Digest, which contains articles, anecdotes, features, and photo essays in a format similar to *Reader's Digest.*

Liguorian, a monthly magazine prepared by the Redemptorist order, contains much of spiritual value.

The Living Light, a quarterly academic journal for teachers, and religious educators.

Missionhurst, Maryknoll, Mountain Spirit, Glenmary Challenge, all report on missionary activity, each focusing on a religious order.

St. Anthony Messenger, which began its 100th year in 1994, reports how faith enriches life and how life enriches faith.

U.S. Catholic, published by the Claretians, deals with issues facing Catholics in their daily lives.

Chicago Studies, published three times a year, contains scholarly studies on various topics such as sacraments, stress, sexuality.

Other specialty magazines are *Church* (ecclesiastics) *Today's Parish* (for parish leadership), *Pastoral Music* (liturgical musicians), *Liturgy 90, Worship, Liturgical Ministry* (liturgy), *Momentum* (Catholic schools), *Religion Teacher's Journal* (catechetics), *Catholic Health* (health and wellness), and *YOU* (youth). Among newsletters is the *Catholic Update,* a four-page, letter-size monthly covering topics of interest to Catholics.

Pro-Life
Rites and liturgy
Sacraments
Sexuality
Stewardship
Stories and songs for children
Vatican II
Vocations
Youth ministry

Include a selection of Catholic magazines, newspapers, and newsletters (see page 73).

A valuable addition to every parish library are booklets in the Ministry Series, published by The Liturgical Press:

The Ministry to the Aging
The Ministry of Believers
The Ministry of the Cantor
The Ministry of Communion
The Liturgical Ministry of Deacons
The Ministry to Persons with Disabilities
The Ministry to the Divorced
The Ministry of Evangelization
The Ministry of Hospitality
The Ministry to the Imprisoned
The Ministry of Lectors
The Ministry of Liturgical Environment
The Ministry of Musicians
The Ministry of Parents to Teen-Agers
The Ministry of the Sacristan
The Ministry of Servers
The Ministry of Service
The Ministry to the Single Person
The Ministry of the Small-Group Leader
The Ministry of Ushers
Youth Ministry

The Catholic Digest Book Club provides a selection of books suitable for reference, family reading, and devotions.

Make an appointment with your pastor, bishop, and other church leaders to discuss selections. Check with other parishes, and plan to spend time with the manager of your local Catholic bookstore.

Develop a bookplate that includes the name and address of your parish, with a request that the book be returned.

Keep the library open on a regular basis—a few hours each Sunday, for example. Place a selection of books on a caddie or utility truck to be stationed outside meeting rooms or in locations where church members gather.

Check-out/Check-in System

Devise a system to keep a record of borrowed books. The system could be as simple as a sheet of paper with space for book title, name of client, date borrowed and date returned.

111.11	Author, Initials	
A12p	Title of Book	
Date Loaned	Borrower's Name	Date Returned
———	————	———
———	————	———
———	————	———
———	————	———
———	————	———
———	————	———

A slightly more elaborate system involves an out-and-in card that should be kept with each book. An envelope for the card is pasted on the inside back cover. The card is transferred from this parent envelope to a "books borrowed" file when the book goes out and is returned to the envelope when the book comes back. Envelopes can be found at office or li-

Parish Library Now Open!

Travel through time
and space...

Discuss the Dead Sea Scrolls with an authority

New Titles Include:

Was Paul Perfect?

Spread of Christianity

Lives of the Saints

History of the Diocese

New Testament for Teens

Lord Love You Because I Can't

brary supply stores, along with check-out cards, date-due forms, and helpful tips from your stationer. It is to be hoped that your parish will include a librarian to assist in this project.

Cooperate with the communications committee in publicizing the library.

Promotion for the Parish Library

The successful parish library is kept before the public gaze:

1. The education and formation committee should work with the communications committee in preparing a quarterly flyer featuring new books and acquisitions in the library.

2. It should develop special themes and displays to promote the library.

For example, use the theme, "Books Will Make Your Summer a Picnic." Spread a red and white checkered tablecloth on a table. Place a wicker basket on the cloth and surround it with picnic supplies, cushions, artificial flowers, and a selection of "summer books" from the library. Use a placard to identify each book.

A promotion of children's books might include an assortment of toys and finger paintings.

Books on Bible study might include a map of the holy land, color photographs, a selection of artifacts.

3. Prepare an exhibit for the library bulletin board each month. Follow a theme. For example, select a stylized tree as a focal point. In summer cover the tree with paper leaves, each bearing the name of a book recommended for good reading. In the fall deck the tree with paper "fruit," each bearing the name of a book.

During winter, use icicles and, during December, trim the tree with Christmas ornaments. Use valentines in February, shamrocks in March, and Easter eggs in April, each bearing the name of a book.

4. Request mention of the library in the Sunday bulletin or in general pulpit announcements.

5. Request an article in your church newsletter.

6. Place posters on tripods in locations where church members gather.

Flyer Promoting the Library

Present reasons why parishioners should avail themselves of the church library, in addition to the public library, emphasizing such points as these:

1. The parish library is readily accessible.

2. It is geared to the interests of church members.

3. Parish members see friends and acquaintances there.

4. It's a good place to make new friends.

5. Books are available without charge.

6. Library hours are convenient (be sure that they are).

7. There is no obligation to hurry in returning items.

Place the flyer in church pews and present it in a form that will encourage churchgoers to take it home—for example, print the flyer on heavy paper and offer it as a flyer or bookmark.

A suggested flyer promoting the parish library is reproduced on page 75.

Chapter 5

Family Life

The purpose of a family life committee or team in your parish is to promote wholesome and Christian family life. Persons working in this area should be strong on family values and appreciate the importance of stable homes. Suggested members: parishioners with varied backgrounds and experiences, such as cradle Catholics and converts, singles and divorced persons, newly marrieds and long-time marrieds, seniors, recovering alcoholics or substance abusers, those with varied racial or ethnic backgrounds, those with homebound or disabled members.

Goals

•To promote a rich and fulfilling Christian family life.

•To seek out and solve problems that could weaken or damage family life.

•To assist families with special needs.

•To support families who are grieving.

Objectives

•*To promote a rich and fulfilling Christian family life.*

1. Develop activities to relate family members to the life of the church and the community.

2. Look to the physical well-being of your parish family by sponsoring annual blood pressure checks, hearing/vision tests, or general health fairs.

3. Develop programs of family enrichment.

4. Recognize changes in the parish family.

5. Develop a Catholic Singles group.

6. Assist with programs of marriage preparation.

7. Assist with programs of marriage enrichment.

8. Design programs to help meet special needs of teenagers and young adults.

9. Design programs to address needs of the elderly.

10. Work with worship and spiritual life committee in promoting family worship and prayer.

•*To seek out and solve problems that could weaken or damage family life.*

1. Promote educational programs on alcohol and substance abuse.

2. Promote and interpret help programs such as Places of Refuge (for runaway children and young people), Tough Love (for troubled/angry teens), Latchkey Kids (for unattended children), and programs offered through Catholic Social Services.

3. Provide support for Respect Life activities.

•*To assist families and persons with special needs.*

1. Seek out and promote help programs for single parents, separated, divorced, and widowed Catholics, troubled marriages.

2. Encourage and support families who have members facing employment or career problems.

3. Find ways of enhancing lives of families with disabled or homebound members.

• *To support families who are hurt or grieving.*
1. Cooperate with such support agencies for the bereaved as Alive-Hospice and Alzheimer Support Services.

2. In event of death send a Mass card, extend condolences, and offer help in funeral preparations.

3. Sponsor bereavement classes for those who have lost loved ones.

4. Work with the pastor in interpreting ceremonies and sacraments for the sick or afflicted.

SPECIFIC PROJECTS IN DETAIL

Health Fairs
l. Schedule periodic screenings for blood pressure, vision and hearing, or

2. Join other churches in sponsoring a community-wide Health Fair, which, in addition to blood pressure, vision, and hearing, would offer tests for such malfunctions as glaucoma, breast and cervical cancer, oral diseases, foot problems, tuberculosis, sickle cell anemia, scoliosis, etc.

  A. To conduct screenings, invite participation from such organizations as the Red Cross, the Cancer Society, the Alzheimer's Association, the Arthritis Foundation, the Heart Association, the Easter Seal, the Leukemia Society, and the Lung Association, plus local hospitals, nurses, medical and dental associations.

  B. Recruit doctors, nurses, laboratory technicians, caregivers, counselors, or health specialists from parish membership.

  C. Make pamphlets available or arrange displays, demonstrations, or film showings to provide information on such subjects as exercise and general fitness, nutrition, safety, stress, mental health, CPR, first aid, and accident prevention.

  D. Seek sponsors to underwrite expenses of the health fair.

Family Enrichment
1. Promote observance of special family days such as Valentine's Day, World Marriage Day, Mother's Day, Father's Day.

  A. On Valentine's Day (February 14), or on World Marriage Day (Sunday closest to Valentine's Day, if it is celebrated in your diocese), invite your bishop to offer a special benediction on those about to be married, on those who are married, and on those who have lost their marriage partners through death. Offer gifts of flowers to those who celebrate golden anniversaries. List wedding anniversaries in your parish newsletter.

  B. Mother's Day is a traditional time for the crowning of the statue of the Blessed Virgin Mary. A suggested program for the ceremony is given on page 79.

May Crowning

Selection of Participants: High school teacher selects upcoming freshman girl for the honor of crowning the statue in honor of the Blessed Mother. Elementary School teacher selects first communicant boy and girl to serve as crown bearer and flower girl. Selections should be based on attendance, dedication, behavior, etc., not necessarily grades.

Scheduling the Ceremony: Schedule the ceremony on a Sunday afternoon in May, a month devoted to the Blessed Virgin Mary, or on Mother's Day.

Suggested Procedure:

1. Choir or congregation sings appropriate hymn. (Choose from scores of Mary hymns including *Ave Maria; Hail, Holy Queen; Hail Mary, Gentle Woman; Immaculate Mary; Queen of the Holy Rosary; Mother Dear, Remember Me; Oh, Mary, We Crown Thee with Blossoms Today;* or *Salve Regina.*)

2. *(optional)* Procession of children who have made first holy communion, dressed in first communion clothes. They take places in reserved seats.

3. The three follow who will take part in the ceremony (the one who will crown the statue leads, followed by the crown bearer, then the flower girl). They proceed to the altar and face the priest.

4. *(optional)* Priest blesses the crown.

5. The three children proceed to the statue of the Blessed Mother.

6. The high school girl takes the crown of flowers from the crown bearer and places it on the statue in honor of the Blessed Mother.

7. The flower girl places her flowers at the feet of the statue.

8. The three turn and take their seats.

C. On Father's Day ask parishioners to attend Mass with red carnations (signifying a living father) or white carnations (deceased father). Observe a moment of silent prayer for deceased fathers.

2. Seek out, evaluate, and promote ways of helping family members understand and accept their roles as spouses and parents.

A. Counseling or training programs are available from Catholic Social Services, state and city agencies, and many hospitals, as well as from such community agencies as the American Red Cross, the YMCA, the YWCA, Family and Children's Services, and the United Way.

B. Some also offer training classes in personal growth, personal awareness, and social responsibility. An example is the Red Cross class in "Parenting," which focuses on skills of nurturing and teaching, considered essential to a child's emotional and intellectual growth.

C. Encourage parish leaders to train as presenters of such diocesan programs as the Active Parenting Program, which equips parents with skills needed to face challenges.

3. Schedule a Marriage Encounter Weekend

A. Include conferences, private counseling, prayer, private reflection, interpersonal dialogue, and Mass.

B. Open the program to married couples, engaged couples, divorced, widowed persons.

Marriage Preparation

1. Prepare personal letters for couples preparing for marriage.

2. Cooperate in presenting Pre-Cana classes.

3. Schedule an Engaged Couples Weekend.

A. Cover such topics as self-encounter, communication, finance, sex/sexuality, and spirituality.

B. Each session should be conducted by a married couple and followed by reflection and time for the engaged couple to share privately. Include group discussions for interaction between engaged and married couples.

4. Schedule a similar Engaged Couples Weekend for couples in which one or both have previously been married.

Recognize Changes in the Parish Family

On parish census cards request (optional) notation of birthdays and marriage dates.

A. Enter birthdays on master calendar: Send cards to mark 5th, 10th, 15th, 20th, 25th, etc. Recognize birthdays after 65 with a rose or carnation. Ask your parish computer expert to design a special parish birthday card (see page 126 for a sample).

B. Enter marriage dates on calendar for posting on Valentine's Day (February 14), or on World Marriage Day (Sunday closest to Valentine's Day). A card can be easily designed on computer.

C. Deliver special cards to parents of the newborn and to the newly christened (see page 125 for a sample).

D. Send an appropriate card or pay personal visits to members of the parish who are ill or hospitalized (see page 127 for a sample).

E. Recognize such events in parish family as weddings, retirements, moves to new homes, honors received, or graduations.

Catholic Singles

Develop a singles group to draw single members of the parish together through shared activities.

The group should meet once a month for a combined business and social session. Schedule get-togethers, recreational and cultural outings, excursions. Plan activities with Catholic singles of adjoining parishes.

Needs of Teenagers and Young Adults

Coordinate and promote programs addressing physical, intellectual, and emotional needs of teenagers and young adults (such as CYO and CYA). Involve them in social service. Help them feel part of the parish family.

1. Look into special programs offered through the diocesan office and Catholic Youth Ministry, such as Search for Christian Maturity (for high school juniors and seniors) and a Youth Leadership Workshop (for all high school students).

2. Support the parish in sending delegates to regional and national Catholic youth conferences.

3. Cooperate with other parishes in sponsoring basketball, baseball, softball, volleyball, and roller-skating leagues for the youth of the parish.

Needs of the Elderly

Plan meetings, get-togethers, and excursions for the elderly for spiritual growth and social exchange.

Develop programs that address needs of the elderly. Many hospitals, and health and community agencies offer training courses in the following subjects:

1. Tutoring and job training of retired persons

2. Recreational class sessions in stretching and exercise.

3. Training in nutrition and diet, stress management.

4. Training for family members in care of stroke victims and the sick and elderly.

Schedule a program of free blood pressure checks.

Provide a Personal Drug Information Checklist. The sample on page 82 is designed to be printed on both sides of an 8½ X 10 inch sheet. Fold to fit with forms and policies.

Respect Life

Raise an awareness of the sacredness of life. Launch a letter-writing campaign in support of Pro-Life legislation. Encourage parish members to address current issues that challenge the sacredness of life.

Support Pro-Life representatives as they develop programs fostering chastity among young people, distribution of anti-pornography information, the crisis pregnancy center, the spiritual adoption of unknown, unborn babies, baby showers for unwed mothers, poster and essay contests, Masses for expectant families.

Promote Respect Life Month (October). Invite speakers, spark discussions.

Assist in promoting the Pro-Life concept by arranging displays, distributing literature.

Families and Persons with Special Needs

1. The Single Parent

Seek out and schedule a non-judgmental, caring program for unmarried women and girls who are pregnant. Prepare volunteers to offer positive help by talking, supplying baby

---

Marriage Enrichment

1. Promote such marriage enrichment programs as evenings of renewal and anniversary celebrations.

2. Schedule Marriage Encounter retreats.

3. Sponsor essay contests for students in elementary schools on such topics as "My Parents, My Home," or "How My Home Reflects Love."

Personal Drug Information Checklist

Patient's Name: _____

SS Number: _____

Primary Insurance Carrier: _____

Secondary Ins. Carrier: _____

Pharmacy: _____

Physician: _____

Phone # of Physician: _____

To the pharmacist
Use this form to counsel the patient about medication.

To the patient
Use this form to guide you in seeking information about medications.

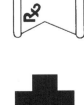

Adapted from "The Right Drug to the Right Patient," copyright 1977, American Pharmaceutical Assn. Prepared in cooperation with APhA.

Rx # _____

Name of Drug: _____

Purpose of Drug: _____

Rx can be renewed _____ times

Take (amount) _____

Every (how often) _____

For (how long) _____

Circle hours drug is to be taken:

1 2 3 4 5 6 7 8 9 10 11 Noon
1 2 3 4 5 6 7 8 9 10 11 Midnight

Physical description of drug: _____

This drug should NOT be taken with: _____

This drug SHOULD be taken with: _____

Possible side effects: _____

Contact your physician or pharmacist if the following side effects occur: _____

Special instructions: _____

Rx # _____

Name of Drug: _____

Purpose of Drug: _____

Rx can be renewed _____ times

Take (amount) _____

Every (how often) _____

For (how long) _____

Circle hours drug is to be taken:

1 2 3 4 5 6 7 8 9 10 11 Noon
1 2 3 4 5 6 7 8 9 10 11 Midnight

Physical description of drug: _____

This drug should NOT be taken with: _____

This drug SHOULD be taken with: _____

Possible side effects: _____

Contact your physician or pharmacist if the following side effects occur: _____

Special instructions: _____

clothes, and by providing resources and referrals. Seek out community training classes on such subjects as parenting, budgeting, self-awareness.

2. Separated, Divorced and Widowed Catholics

These persons are going through a healing process, so programs should provide comfort and help. Speakers and seminars for separated and divorced Catholics are available through agencies of the church, as well as through civic and state counseling services.

3. Troubled Marriages

Seek programs from the diocese to help heal and renew troubled marriages. One such program is the Retrouvaille Weekend, which offers participants a chance to rediscover themselves and their spouses and renew a loving relationship in marriage.

Families with Disabled or Homebound Members

A. Cooperate with the administration and stewardship committee in checking and updating facilities for the disabled. Examples of such adaptations:

- access ramps at building entrances
- rest room adaptations
- Braille plates on elevators
- automatic door openers
- provisions for the hearing impaired.

B. Develop programs to address needs of the disabled and elderly.

(1) Work with your state's Department of Employment Security in vocational testing and job placement.

(2) Provide parish members temporary use of wheelchairs, walking aids, hospital beds.

C. Schedule classes in such help programs as Stretchercise (mild exercise), and Adapted Aquatics (water exercise and swim programs for the disabled). Make arrangements for transportation to class sites.

D. Work with schools to direct children in preparing and distributing remembrances to the isolated or homebound.

E. Begin a program of sending cards, letters, or church bulletins to homebound persons on a regular basis.

Bereavement

Oftentimes it helps to share grief. It is beneficial to talk about loss to someone who also has suffered loss. In a bereavement class, members find comfort by talking with one another about dying and living, loss and gain, memories sad and happy. The class is monitored by a counselor who assists participants in their process of healing.

Members of the parish may want to bring comfort to those suffering loss but don't know how. The family life committee might suggest Mass cards, bereavement cards, a visit to the funeral home, an offer to run errands, an offer of overnight lodging for out-of-town family members, coordination of an evening meal for the family or preparation of a special dish. An act of special thoughtfulness: Offer to have family vehicle washed and waxed for the funeral procession.

F. Note that, by law, Seeing Eye dogs (leather harness) or Hearing Ear dogs (orange harness) must be admitted to public buildings. Ushers should be made aware of this.

Ceremonies and Sacraments for the Sick and Afflicted

At least two church ceremonies and sacraments are conducted especially for the sick and afflicted, but all members of the parish should be encouraged to attend. The ceremonies are:

1. The devotion to St. Blaise on his feast day February 3, including blessing of throats

2. The Anointing of the Sick. According to the "Rite of Anointing and Pastoral Care of the Sick," those receiving this sacrament are:

• the sick and elderly whose health is seriously impaired

• those about to undergo surgery

• elderly persons with weakened health

• sick children who are mature enough to be comforted by the sacrament

Chapter 6

Parish Life

A strong parish life committee will support the life of your parish, bring church members together, and help you reach out to the alienated and unchurched.

This work calls for persons who have a good understanding of parish life. Look for possible candidates among RCIA team members, Legion of Mary members, deacons, service providers, recreation workers, teachers, organizers, good listeners and communicators, and members of the Holy Name Society.

Goals

•To support the life of the parish through special events and celebrations, and to help draw families together through shared activities.

•To explore ways to involve more church members in activities of the parish.

•To reach out to the alienated and unchurched.

•To extend programs to parishioners confined to their homes or who are in medical or health service facilities.

•To seek out ways to make newcomers feel welcome.

•To build a sense of "belonging" among members of the parish.

Objectives

• *To support the life of the parish through special events and celebrations, and to help draw families together through shared activities.*

1. Sponsor fellowship coffees each Sunday.

2. Sponsor parish family nights.

3. Sponsor excursions and field trips to nearby religious sites, sister parishes, and places of interest.

4. Contribute to the social and recreational needs of all parishioners: children, youth, newcomers, families, single adults, seniors, other specialized groups.

   A. Schedule an outdoor picnic for members of the parish at least once a year.

   B. Coordinate an annual open house. If the open house takes place in the education/activities building it provides opportunity for new acquaintances and friendships. If given in the rectory it provides opportunity to view the clergy from a more personal viewpoint.

5. Work with other churches and civic groups in meeting social needs of the community.

• *To explore ways to involve more church members in activities of the parish.*

1. Plan activities that are appropriate and of interest to all members of the parish.

2. Give activities adequate publicity, explanation, and interpretation.

3. See that all parishioners know that they are invited.

4. Those responding should be welcomed and made to feel part of the group.

5. Maintain an active talent file of parish members. Include all types of skills and talents.

6. Cooperate with the worship and spiritual life committee in selecting gift bearers.

• *To reach out to the alienated and the unchurched.*
1. Work with a social action committee in sponsoring food pantries, homeless shelters, and emergency lodgings (see Chapter 7).

2. Work with family life committee in providing support and referrals to individuals and families affected by alcohol and drug abuse (see Chapter 5).

3. Work with the social action committee in ministry to the imprisoned. A good source of help is *The Ministry to the Imprisoned*, published by The Liturgical Press.

• *To extend programs to parishioners confined to their homes or who are in medical or health service facilities.*
1. Coordinate a visitation program for the homebound, disabled, ill, and elderly.

2. Coordinate a transportation program for the elderly and the handicapped.

• *To seek out ways to make newcomers feel welcome.*

1. Set up a program of newcomer contact.

2. Set up a newcomer table.

3. Sponsor an annual Hospitality Sunday for newcomers.

• *To build a sense of "belonging" among members of the parish.*

1. Cooperate with the communications committee in distributing a roster or directory of parish members.

2. Design programs and activities for specific age and gender groups such as:
    Children
    Junior Catholic Youth
    Senior Catholic Youth
    Men of the church
    Women of the church
    Marrieds
    Singles
    Parents
    The elderly

3. Encourage parishioners to take an active part in church life: join the choir, attend parish coffees, turn out for the bloodmobile, support the church rummage/craft sales, sign up to help in the Habitat for Humanity building project, teach a church school class, join the prayer network, be an usher, etc.

SPECIFIC PROJECTS IN DETAIL

Fellowship Coffees

"Coffees" have become standard Sunday features at most churches, thanks to time-pressed congregations and a universal appreciation for the coffee bean. Families gather to enjoy a cup, meet friends, and greet newcomers, then hurry on about their business.

Designate a place and a time, find a commercial urn, and send out for a pound of regular ground.

To make coffee lovers happy don't use powdered creamers. Individual containers of Half-and-Half can be obtained in lots of a thousand from dairies or food wholesalers.

Some sippers are cautious of styrofoam, so offer paper hot-cups as well.

Of course, things would be nicer if you used linen, china, and home baked breads (but, then, a string quartet and orchids for the ladies wouldn't be bad, either).

Parish Family Nights

Suggested Dates: every 4th Thursday

Suggested Times: 7:00 P.M. to 9:00 P.M.

Suggested Menu: soup and salad. If you decide to offer more elaborate meals, many books are available to guide your kitchen crew in preparing food in quantity. Here are two of them: *Food for Fifty*, by Grace Shugart and Mary Mott (Macmillan); *Cooking for Fifty,* by Chet Holden, (John Wiley & Sons).

Suggested Themes for Parish Family Nights:

- "Health" Lecture, video, literature, displays on such topics as weight control, exercise, nutrition, stress, stroke, hypertension.

- "Missions" Report, photographs or video on parish's adopted mission. Include artifacts, souvenirs from mission field.

- "The Papal Flag, the State Flag, the U.S.

The secret of good coffee? Abide by these four rules:

1. Start with a clean coffee maker. Tackle dark deposits with steel wool and baking soda. (Use cleaning powders with caution because they could affect taste.) After a thorough cleaning, soak pot and elements in water and baking soda until clean and scent free.

2. Select fine grind coffee for drip-style maker; urn or perk grind for percolator.

3. Use filtered water but remove impurities such as chlorine and chemicals only. One guru of the bean declares, "the harder the water the better the coffee."

4. Employ proper measurements. Controversy rages over exact proportions but those listed below are safe:

2 oz coffee	regular grind,	+ 1 gal water	= 12	8-oz cups
4 oz coffee	regular grind	+ 2 gal water	= 24	8 oz cups
1 lb coffee	regular grind	+ 8 gal water	= 50	8 oz cups
1.5 lb coffee	regular grind	+ 12 gal water	= 90	8 oz cups

For a special treat, place one/three sticks of cinnamon atop coffee grounds.

Flag." Study flag history, etiquette. Present a flag to the church.

- "International Night." Tables assigned various nationalities. Emphasis on heritage, customs, costumes, beauty of country-side, dishes.
- "Storytelling." Invite a storyteller to tell Bible stories or spin tales for the young and young-at-heart.
- "Thursday Night at the Movies." Suggest "Going My Way," "Boy's Town," or other family picture. Admission: gift for patient at local nursing home.

Parish Excursions

In your city or within a few miles of it are many historic attractions, notable buildings, gardens, parks, museums, galleries, even shopping malls. Also there are a number of religious sites and other parishes of interest. Most of these locations have never been visited by many persons in your parish. Many parishioners lack transportation, are afraid to travel alone, or simply never get around to it.

On the other hand, in your city are many bus companies, transit firms, or charter services who are waiting to provide transportation at a reasonable fee.

Select a destination and make a visit of inspection. Request group rates for admission. Reserve a comfortable bus with wide windows and a clean rest room. Add expenses together (remembering a tip for the bus driver) and divide by the number of bus seats (approximately 46 to 60). The result: the cost per guest for your first parish bus excursion.

A few tips. Be sure the bus company carries adequate liability insurance. Make an advance run to check out handicap access, rest room fa-

cilities, availability of guides, and to arrive at a time estimate. Also, you will want to gather pamphlets for distribution. Arrange for box lunches (add to overall price) or seek out a good restaurant and allow time for a lunch break. Reproduce a brief itinerary. Finally, present each guest a small souvenir of the outing.

Outdoor Picnic

Appoint committees for site selection, food preparation, beverages, serving, recreation, clean up, publicity.

1. Site Selection: Look for a convenient location. The site should be safe for children and feature adequate parking, clean rest room facilities, handicap access, overhead shelter in event of rain, and a playground. Make advance reservations if necessary. In addition, someone should go to the site at least two hours in advance to "hold" it. Appoint someone to prepare signs pointing the way, to be placed at intersections as needed. In addition, print directions to the site in the church bulletin.

2. Food Preparation: A convenient plan is to provide the entree and ask parishioners to bring vegetable dishes to share. Appoint a "cook & grill" team. Make someone responsible for tablecloths, cups, glasses, napkins, knives and forks, and condiments.

3. Serving Teams: Teams should check-in covered dishes as they arrive, place food on the table, provide serving spoons, and assist in serving plates from the grill.

4. Beverages: Coffee for forty, anyone? You will need a giant coffee maker, plus sugar/sweetener and cream. Tea, hot or iced? Bring tubs of ice for soft drinks.

5. Recreation: Remember to bring sports equip-

ment. You will need balls in at least three sizes, gloves, bats, nets. If there's water be sure to bring safety equipment. Supplies at every church outing should include a first aid kit and someone to use it properly.

6. Clean-up: Provide refuse cans. Reserve at least one for soft drink cans and other recyclable items. At the close of the outing distribute plastic bags and ask everyone to help police the area. In addition, have a clean-up crew standing by.

7. Publicity: Get the word out for a strong turnout. Notify your communications committee early for help in promotion. See that a notice appears in the church bulletin. Place flyers in pews and posters on bulletin boards.

Talent File

Seek out skills, talents, and special interests by sending out a questionnaire or by requesting information while conducting the parish census. Make parishioners aware of volunteer opportunities available to them. List and describe jobs in a flyer or pamphlet.

See Appendix A for a Census/Skills/Interest Form. Each church task has been given a number, keyed to assignments outlined in this book.

Begin a Visitation Program for the Homebound, Ill, and Elderly

1. Assemble a list of parishioners to be visited. Include the elderly, the disabled, the homebound, the hospitalized, and retirement home/nursing home residents.

2. Seek out what patients need. Is a visitor needed to read, to talk, to listen, or simply to serve as a caring presence?

3. Recruit volunteers via pulpit announcements, newsletter appeals, telephone tree, posters, flyers, and word of mouth.

4. Schedule training. Speakers are available from many hospitals, Red Cross, and United Way services. Set up a model hospital room so trainees can play act and critique.

5. Print the following rules on a sheet of paper and ask trainees to study and abide by them.

Rx For Hospital Visitors

A. Observe visiting hours. Follow rules regarding number of visitors.

B. Keep visits brief.

C. Observe smoking regulations.

D. No loud noises.

E. Sit where the patient can see without straining. Sitting on the patient's bed is a no-no.

F. Be careful of interruptions. The considerate visitor who arrives in the middle of a favorite TV show, for example, will delay conversation until the program is ended.

G. Do not criticize facilities, staff, or medical treatment, and refrain from relating any "hospital of horror" experiences.

H. Ask if patient needs water pitcher filled, bed adjusted, pillow fluffed, photographs or flowers moved into view, or other service.

I. Bring with you a church bulletin, a parish newsletter, reading material, TV guide, flowers, photographs. Check with nurse before presenting food, especially candy.

Transportation Program

1. Determine needs of those who need assistance, such as errands done, meals delivered, or transportation for shopping, doctor or clinic visits, trips to bank or post office, or "just to get outside."

Many stores feature substantial discounts for seniors on specific days of the week. Remember these days in arranging transportation for elderly shoppers.

The Meals on Wheels program, which delivers meals to the homebound, is conducted in cooperation with other churches in the community.

Screening Drivers

Potential drivers should be screened to assure that only capable drivers operate vehicles on behalf of your parish. Your diocesan office probably will have necessary forms. If not, seek answers to such questions as:

1. Are you at least 18 years of age?

2. Do you have a valid drivers license?

3. Have you ever been cited for unsafe driving?

4. Do you carry $500,000 combined single limit liability insurance covering property damage and bodily injury?

Many churches request Motor Vehicle Reports on potential drivers as a matter of routine. The reports, which show if a person has been convicted of a driving offense, can usually be obtained from your State Department of Safety (or its equivalent) for a fee. To get the information you will need the applicant's date of birth, operator's license number, and Social Security number.

---

2. Recruit, screen, and train volunteers to provide vehicles and transportation.

Many states require a chauffeur's license for those operating buses or vans carrying passengers.

Newcomer Contact

Make newcomers feel wanted with a newcomer packet. Ideally, these packets would be distributed during home visits.

Twin-pocket portfolios are available in colors and can be printed with the name and a photograph of your church. Prepare pages in graded sizes for placement in pockets so readers will see the "total picture" as they open the packets.

Suggested contents of newcomer packet:

1. Letter of welcome, signed by pastor.

2. Directory of parish groups and organizations, accompanied by pamphlets on such groups as the parish pastoral council, the RCIA, the Altar Society, the Legion of Mary, the St. Vincent de Paul Society, the Diocesan Council of Catholic Women, the Catholic Youth Organization, the Knights of Columbus.

3. List of volunteer opportunities with sign-up form

4. Calendar of Parish activities

5. Current issue of parish newsletter

As an aid in seeking out newcomers, prepare a visitor card to be placed in a rack inside the church entrance and in pews. Also, ushers might hand out cards to those they recognize as newcomers.

A suggested visitor card is shown at the top of the next page: Reproduce on stock to fit a 5 X 4 inch file drawer.

A suggested visitor card.

WELCOME, VISITORS!

Please complete this card if you wish a personal visit or want to be added to our church mailing list.

(Name)_____

(Home Phone)_____ (Work Phone) _____

(Address) _____

Are you a newcomer to this diocese?   ❑ Yes ❑ No

Are you a member of the Catholic church?   ❑ Yes ❑ No

Would you like a layperson to visit?   ❑ Yes ❑ No

(Please phone the church office if you want to see a priest)

May we add your name to our mailing list?   ❑ Yes ❑ No

May we notify you of our next Open House?   ❑ Yes ❑ No

---

1. Act on information obtained from these cards. Obtain additional newcomer information from the church office.

See that each individual or family is contacted by visit, telephone call, or mail. Give each person a newcomer packet.

2. Set aside a newcomer table at parish functions.

At parish dinners, coffees, or seated get-togethers, designate a special table for newcomers. Seek newcomers out for welcome and fellowship.

3. Schedule a Hospitality Sunday at least twice a year.

The purpose of Hospitality Sunday is to encourage the parish to make newcomers feel welcome and urge them to take part in church programs and activities.

4. Conduct a program of home visitation for new families.

Programs for Specific Age and Gender Groups

Activities for Children

Every child should have opportunity to view the world as a place of wonder and delight. Seasonal activities sponsored by the family life committee will bring no small amount of happiness to children of the parish. At the same time, the activities will serve to bring families together for warmth and fellowship.

Develop activities for each season. A few examples:

1. Christmas: Allow children to bring clusters of straw for the parish manger scene; help them prepare advent wreaths; ask them to bring wrapped gifts to be presented to children of impoverished families (through the social action committee); arrange to send greeting

cards to children in mission churches; suggest that children make a gift of books to the parish lending library; let them prepare decorations for a parish Christmas tree.

2. Valentine's Day: Help children prepare valentines.

3. St Patrick's Day: Give children small, potted shamrock plants (botanical name, Oxalis) with instructions for care and watering.

4. Easter: Let children gather for a retelling of the Easter story; set up a rabbit petting zoo; sponsor an egg-coloring contest (winners based on originality, artistic excellence, and appropriateness); set up an egg tree; arrange for an egg hunt; plan an Easter parade of homemade hats and bonnets.

5. Independence Day: Distribute to children of the parish small American flags or liberty bells. Bells can be found at stores selling crafts, pet supply, and hobby shops.

6. Halloween: After Mass on All Saints Day, November 1 (a holy day of obligation that honors all Christian saints), assemble children for a review of some of our best known saints; sponsor a pumpkin carving class, an apple bobbing contest, or a costume party.

7. St. Francis of Assisi: During the week of October 4, birthday of St. Francis, sponsor an outdoor "Blessing of the Animals." Invite children to bring their pets. Suggested tie-ins: demonstration of working animals such as Seeing Eye or Hearing Ear dogs, demonstrations of obedience training by local canine groups. If there is a veterinarian in your congregation, ask him or her to offer suggestions for pet care, perhaps offer inoculations at a reduced price. A pet medallion, offered by Roman, Inc., is available

from many religious book stores and hospital gift shops or from Cat Claws (1004 West Broadway, P.O. Box 1001, Morrilton, AR 72110; 1-800-783-0977). It is made of pewter, is about the size of a 50 cent piece, and comes in a presentation folder which includes a prayer to St. Francis.

8. Catholic School Week (usually at the end of January or beginning of February): Children choose a saint to represent, give clues, and answer questions to determine identity. During Mass on first Sunday in February reserve section for teachers or for school students.

Junior Catholic Youth Organization for 7th and 8th grade students

Meets monthly during school year for recreational and service programs. Members participate in such activities as hay rides, skating and swim parties, pizza feasts, and assist in programs to benefit the parish and the community. They fund projects through such schemes as potted plant, T-shirt and Easter egg sales, car wash and windshield cleanings.

Senior CYO for 9th through 12th grade students.

Meets monthly during school year to promote life as Christians by developing self-awareness, participating in recreational activities, conducting workshops, and assisting in programs to benefit the parish and the community such as Habitat for Humanity, toys for tots, the shelter program, the food kitchen. Activities include Christmas caroling, bowling, canoe trips, dances, hay rides, hikes, picnics, ice skating, and rafting. Members hold retreats, vespers, workshops. They raise money for projects through bake and handcraft sales, garage sales, car washes.

Men's Club

All men of the parish are considered part of the Men's Club, which serves the church while providing fellowship to its members. Among programs: Christmas baskets and toys for families in need, shelter and food programs, Habitat for Humanity, coaching and supervising CYO sports programs.

Women's Groups

Mother Clubs meet monthly, offer programs of special interest to moms. Members sponsor a weekday nursery or baby-sitting service for "Mother's Day Out." Those who can sew gather to create tapestries and kneeler pads, repair vestments and clerical linens. Begin a Catholic Business Women group. Women of every church are invited to join the Diocesan Council of Catholic Women (DCCW).

Both Men and women gather for social and recreational events: bridge and canasta parties, golf/bowling leagues, travel, bingo.

Chapter 7

Social Action

A social action team or committee works to promote and interpret the church's teaching about social issues and to involve parishioners in helping to meet the social needs of their community.

Committee Members

Look for parishioners interested in social ministry, members of Ladies of Charity, Legion of Mary, Holy Name Society, St. Vincent dePaul society, DCCW, prison ministry, those wishing to assist the homeless, destitute, or illiterate.

Goals

•To define problems and community issues that can be addressed by the social action committee.

•To raise consciousness about social needs and issues.

•To involve parishioners in social ministry.

•To support and cooperate with such organizations as Ladies of Charity, the "Room in the Inn" program, St. Vincent dePaul Society and the "Loaves & Fishes" program.

Objectives

• *To define problems and community issues that can be addressed by the social action committee.*
1. Schedule a meeting of representatives from key welfare agencies, the Holy Name Society,

St. Vincent dePaul Society, prison ministry, the United Way or its equivalent, the state Department of Human Welfare, the Salvation Army, and other agencies devoted to social action.

A. Select at least four major problems or community issues needing attention. Examples of such problems or community issues:

  Adult illiteracy
  Blood/tissue shortage
  Campaign for Human Development
  Children home without supervision (Latchkey kids)
  Children abandoned
  Crime Increase
  Drug/Alcohol/Substance abuse
  Energy sources for the destitute
  Housing for low income families
  Juvenile delinquency
  Prison reform and ministry to the imprisoned
  Retarded/handicapped needing assistance
  Safe havens for battered spouses
  Safe havens for runaway children
  Safe havens for pregnant singles
  Sex education
  Sexually transmitted diseases
  Shelters for the poor and homeless
  Transportation for elderly/handicapped
  Visitation to hospitalized/shut-ins

Visitation to elderly

Voter registration

World Hunger

B. Select four issues for the attention of the social action committee.

• *To involve parishioners in social ministry.*

1. Determine how the social action committee can best deal with the community issues or problems outlined above.

A. For example, if one of the problems selected is a shortage of blood, set up a program of blood donor recruitment.

B. If a problem is literacy, organize an adult literacy program.

C. Lack of housing for low-income families is a problem in most areas. Investigate the Habitat for Humanity program. Labor is contributed, as are land and building materials. Approximately 300 volunteers are necessary to build a typical house.

D. If juvenile delinquency is a problem in your community, consider sponsoring a Scouting program.

E. If shelter for the homeless is a major problem, organize a shelter program in which other community churches are invited to participate.

SPECIFIC PROJECTS IN DETAIL

Blood Donor Recruitment

As members of your parish consider a blood drive, they might review the following facts and figures:

Someone needs blood every two minutes. During the time it takes for a bloodmobile visit (approximately three hours) more than ninety persons will need blood transfusions.

Sixty percent of the people are eligible to give blood, but less than four percent actually donate.

Sixty-seven percent of blood donors make only one donation a year. Only about one in ten gives three times but a person can give as often as six times a year (or every 56 days).

Male blood donors outnumber female donors by more than two to one (8 percent vs 2.9 percent).

There is a 97.6 percent likelihood that anyone who lives to age 72 will require a blood transfusion at some time.

With each transfusion episode the average patient receives 3.4 units of blood. According to the *Guinness Book of World Records*, the biggest blood transfusion ever received was 2,400 pints—given in 1970 to a heart surgery patient in Chicago.

When a person donates a pint of blood the body reproduces the fluid in about 24 hours.

To make a blood donation a person must be 17 years of age or older, and weigh at least 110 pounds. There is no age cutoff. People can give as long as they are healthy.

Organizing a Bloodmobile Visit

1. Obtain sanction for participation from pastor and parish council.

2. Work with representatives of local blood collection agency, such as the American Red Cross. Do these things:

A. Agree on a goal for the parish blood drive.

B. Agree on a date.

C. Choose mode of collection:

(1) Bloodmobile visit: The agency sends a team to set up a collection site in your building or dispatches a self-contained unit to be stationed outside in your parking area.

(2) Seek commitments from parishioners to visit the local blood center. In some instances provide transportation for them.

3. Recruit volunteers to receive orientation and training.

4. The training program will follow these lines:
   A. Explain need. Outline procedures for conducting mobile visit or seeking commitments to donate.

B. Show blood program film provided by blood program representative

C. Divide workers into committees:

(1) Publicity committee to publicize the drive, make announcements, prepare news releases, put up posters, and distribute flyers.

(2) Telephone recruitment committee to call prospects and seek commitments.

(3) On-site Bloodmobile aides, such as volunteers to handle reception, registration, canteen, or motor corps, plus nurses for the donor room.

Adult Literacy

First, determine the need. Which of the categories listed below does your parish wish to serve:

1. Illiterate adults, i.e., persons who are unable to read or write. For full information call the National Institute for Literacy, telephone 1-800-228-8813.

2. Literate persons who are unable to read or speak English. Call Laubach Literacy, telephone 315-445-8000.

A number of different texts are available for the "English as a Second Language" (ESL) program. Write Heinle Publishers, Wadsworth, Inc., Boston MA 02116; Linmore Publishers, Box 1545, Palatine, IL 60098; or Addison-Wesley Publishing, 1 Jacob Way, Reading, MA 01867.

An excellent corollary of the ESL program is the *Oxford Picture Dictionary*, Oxford University Press, 200 Madison Avenue, New York, N.Y. 10016.

Literacy programs and refugee resettlement programs, because of their scope and size, frequently are tackled on a multi-parish or interdenominational basis. Catholic Charities and a number of community agencies are often involved, as are scores of volunteer workers.

For the ESL program you will need to seek out a meeting place, decide on text and teaching materials, recruit and train instructors and workers, get word of the program to potential clients, and, if necessary, arrange transportation to and from class sessions.

D. Separate groups into units for training. Set deadlines.

5. Each committee will complete jobs as assigned.

Habitat for Humanity

Many people live in substandard housing. Your parish can take action by sponsoring construction of a Habitat for Humanity home.

Your people will work side by side with the selected family in constructing the home. Parishes can be united, perhaps as never before, by this life-giving partnership.

The Habitat for Humanity program, "building homes in partnership with God's people in need," is a nonprofit ecumenical housing ministry that helps needy families get decent housing. Each house costs about $40,000 but the sponsor can reduce the amount by providing in-kind contributions of materials and services. Families who qualify can purchase homes at cost. They pay the price back over a twenty-year period with no interest. Monthly payments are about $250, including taxes and insurance.

House design and construction are overseen by a building committee, which consults the family about their housing needs. Houses are simple, single-family structures, varying from 900 to 1,100 square feet with central heat and air. Homes are equipped with simple kitchens that include a stove and refrigerator.

Houses are built by volunteers and the future homeowners. It usually takes a minimum of twenty workers a day to construct a Habitat house, not including the professionals who handle technical jobs. Homes are built in one of three ways:

1. Eight consecutive days, Saturday through Saturday.

2. Four weekends with volunteers working Saturday and Sunday each week.

3. Eight consecutive Saturdays.

The Habitat for Humanity program orders all materials and handles inspections and subcontracting. In advance of construction the building committee meets with the sponsor to organize volunteers. Representatives coordinate each day's activity at the construction site. Insurance prohibits anyone under the age of 16 from being on the construction site.

Former President Jimmy Carter, after taking part in the program, said, "The sacrifice I thought I would be making turned out to be one of the greatest blessings of my life." He said the program vividly demonstrates the adage, "love in action."

Scouting

As Girl Scout Founder Juliette Gordon Low pointed out more than eighty years ago, the "character" of our nation is a strong reflection of the values we teach our young people. Good citizens are nurtured at an early age. Through Scouting, boys and girls make solid friendships, learn respect for self and others, develop life skills, and grow in moral, physical, and emotional strength. Programs have been developed for every age, from kindergarten through the terrible teens.

Cub and Boy Scouts are active with community service projects, merit badge work, camping, and outings. The older Scout Varsity teams and Explorer posts are involved in civic and community service.

Daisy (girls of kindergarten age), Brownie, and Junior Girl Scout troops learn good citizenship, and receive guidance in moral and emotional growth. Cadette and Senior Girl

Scouts learn skills to guide them through changing cultural and social roles.

Every troop needs a sponsor:

1. To secure a meeting place for its troop.

2. To help recruit strong resource people to serve as members of the troop committee.

3. To help provide a well-rounded program.

To learn how your parish can sponsor a Scout troop, call the office of your Boy or Girl Scout council.

Winter Shelter Program

The Room in the Inn program is a way of providing a community's homeless population a warm and safe sleeping place during winter months.

Ideally, families are given transportation to the shelter site, are served a hot dinner, offered a magazine or book to read or television to watch, and provided soap and fresh towels, plus clean sheets and a pillowcase. In the morning guests are served breakfast and given sack lunches. At Christmas time each person is given a backpack or gym bag filled with toiletries and clothing, plus toys for the children.

Some churches provide changing tables, hygiene programs, a separate area for those recovering from addictions, an adult literacy program, or a "Step-Out" plan to help guests find jobs and housing.

Among volunteers needed for a winter shelter program:

1. "Innkeepers" to stay overnight with guests.

2. Cooks and food handlers to prepare and serve meals.

3. Laundry teams to wash and dry sheets, linens, and towels.

4. Drivers to provide transportation for shelter guests.

5. Contributors of children's toys, Christmas gifts, and money to fund program.

On the following page is a promotional piece about a shelter for the homeless. It explains the program in detail.

Room in the Inn
at the Cathedral

Room in the Inn

We are about to enter our seventh year of Room in the Inn at the Cathedral!

Room in the Inn was founded by Father Charles Strobel as a way of keeping our homeless population in Nashville warm and safe at night during the winter months. Over the years it has grown from just a few to over a hundred participating congregations throughout the city. Many new services have been added as well, such as a shower and hygiene program, a "Guest House" (for people recovering from addictions, "Step-Out" to help people get back into jobs and housing, a literacy program, and several other programs begun just last year.

We'd like to tell you just how Room in the Inn works at the Cathedral!

We have many teams, each fulfilling its particular responsibility to make the program run smoothly and efficiently. The sign-up sheet, on the reverse side, details the duties of each team.

On Tuesday nights at 6:30 our drivers meet at St. Albert Hall and leave for Room in the Inn center at 6th and Demonbreun where they pick up our twenty guests (we take both men and women) and bring them to the church. We serve them a hot dinner, offer them a book or a magazine to read or TV for those who wish to watch it. They bed down for the night in St. Albert Hall on air mattresses.

In the morning they are awakened at 5:45, fed breakfast, and lunches are given to be taken with them. The drivers arrive at 6:30 to return the guests to the downtown center. The innkeepers clean up the area and lock up the hall. A laundry team member picks up the linens to wash and return before the following Tuesday.

After six years, the program is operating very well and we have been very pleased with the generous and enthusiastic participation by the Cathedral parishioners, all who seen to enjoy the effort and derive much satisfaction from it.

In all these six winters we have never had a serious problem with our guests. They have been pleasant, thoughtful, grateful people, many of whom request the Cathedral because they feel welcome and comfortable here.

Please consider joining us this year. We run from November through March. If you have any questions, call Kristy Dixon (555-2973) or Jim Coode (555-8349). Or if you know someone who has participated in this capacity, give them a call and ask about their experience.

Chapter 8

Worship and Spiritual Life

A worship and spiritual life committee cooperates with the pastor, staff, and other parish groups to help build the parish's liturgical, devotional, and prayer life.

Suggested Committee Members

Representatives of groups dealing with spiritual life, including members of the Legion of Mary, Knights of Columbus, Cursillo, religious education workers, deacons, and participants in the parish prayer network.

Goals

• To initiate programs to help all members of the parish participate in liturgical celebrations.

• To plan liturgical celebrations.

• To cooperate with other parish groups in providing care for the church and its furnishings.

• To encourage vocations.

• To cooperate with other denominations in conducting programs of worship and spiritual life.

• To support the Legion of Mary and to cooperate with the parish life committee in offering supportive programs.

Objectives

• *To initiate programs to help all members of the parish participate in liturgical celebrations.*

1. Help create a proper environment for worship.

2. Help prepare parishioners to take part in liturgical celebrations.

3. Assist in recruiting ministers of communion (eucharistic ministers).

4. Select gift bearers.

5. Assist in selecting and training lectors and commentators.

6. Assist in recruiting and selecting cantors.

7. Help train and supervise altar servers, acolytes.

8. Assist in recruiting and training ushers.

9. Sustain and assist music directors, organist, and choir as they prepare for liturgy.

10. Support and assist the bellringer choir.

• *To plan liturgical celebrations*

1. Evaluate programs involved in the spiritual development of the parish.

2. Plan liturgical celebrations to meet spiritual needs of parishioners.

  A. Schedule a children's liturgy of the word each Sunday.

  B. Schedule at least four spiritual retreats a year for members of the parish.

  C. Institute prayer programs.

  D. Organize a prayer network.

3. Work with the ministry staff in enriching prayer experience.

• *To cooperate with other parish societies and committees in providing for the care of the church and its furnishings.*
1. Work with the church altar society in coordinating a program of altar flowers at every worship service.

2. Assist in training the sacristan.

3. Work with building and grounds committee in maintaining outdoor shrines, grottoes, stations of the cross.

• *To encourage vocations in all walks of life: ordained ministry, religious life, single or married life.*
1. Promote First Thursday prayers for vocations to the priesthood and religious life. Promote observance of the World Day of Prayer for Vocations on the Fourth Sunday of Easter.

2. Arrange speaking engagements and newsletter articles by those entering or about to enter the ministry, emphasizing why they have chosen this way of life.

• *To cooperate with other denominations in conducting programs of worship and spiritual life and to promote and participate in programs with churches of other denominations.*
1. Visit churches of other denominations and invite visits in turn.

2. Cooperate with churches of other denominations in such areas as the shelter program, Meals on Wheels, Habitat for Humanity, adult literacy, safe havens (see Chapter 7).

• *To support the Legion of Mary.*
1. By interpreting the Legion of Mary's lay ministry programs to the homebound, the sick, and the infirm.

2. By cooperating with the committee on parish life by offering supportive visitation programs as needed.

SPECIFIC PROJECTS IN DETAIL

Help Create a Proper Environment for Worship

The upper room prepared for Christ and his disciples was "furnished and all in order" (Mark 14:15). Take a look at the liturgical environment of your church. Is all in order?

Environment includes all that touches the eye and ear, the tastes and odors, the temperature and texture, the presence of space. Taking all factors into consideration, a proper liturgical environment means a comfortable and spacious place to worship.

1. Be sure that your seating spaces are favorable to a reverent atmosphere.

  A. As much as possible, is the seating of the

church arranged around the altar so the people have a sense of "gathering around the table" with the Lord?

B. Are pews spaced to enable people to sit without crowding? Is there room to kneel comfortably?

C. Are seats and kneelers provided with cushions?

D. Is someone assigned to tidy pews between Masses, removing discarded papers and placing literature in appropriate racks?

2. Work with your sacristan or altar committee to see that sacred vessels and furnishings are clean and polished, and that altar linens and vestments are clean, neat, and conducive to worship.

3. Prepare a printed schedule of each Mass, listing the order of service, hymn numbers, and the titles of special music selections.

4. Prepare a printed schedule of Masses and other services during each season of the liturgical year. Encourage parishioners to take copies home to keep for reference.

Members of every Catholic congregation should be provided missalettes to guide their participation in the worship service. Be sure that enough are on hand. Missalettes can be ordered from a number of religious publishers, among them the J. S. Paluch Company in Chicago, St. Paul Book & Media in Boston, the Oregon Catholic Press in Portland, the Leaflet Missal Company in St. Paul, or World Library in Schiller Park, IL.

Among sources for altar bread is the Meyer-Vogelpohl Bakery, 717 Race Street, Cincinnati, Ohio 45202; 1-800-543-0264. Other sources for altar bread are listed in the advertising section

of the Official Catholic Directory.

The Directory also lists companies offering such liturgical supplies as altar linens, church candles, processional and hanging crosses, sacred vessels, albs, cassocks, and vestments.

Assist in Recruiting Ministers of Communion (Eucharistic Ministers)

1. Insert recruitment appeal for eucharistic ministers in Sunday bulletin.

2. Ask that an appeal be made through the prayer network.

3. Request an appeal from the pulpit.

4. Post an appeal on the parish bulletin board.

5. Prepare a letter of appeal for parish groups and organizations.

6. Submit an article to the parish newsletter explaining the need for eucharistic ministers.

7. Make available *The Ministry of Communion*, by Michael Kwatera, O.S.B. (Liturgical Press). Place booklet in the parish library; include it in your literature rack.

Gift Bearers

If parishioners mention that they sit next to people for years and never learn their names, it is time to take some sort of action. A partial solution is the expansion of the gift bearer program.

Meet with your priest to develop guidelines. For example, which Masses and which special days have gift bearers? How are bearers selected? Will persons be asked to serve if their spouses belong to other churches? Are children invited to accompany their parents?

In one successful program the gift bearer committee meets once a month to place telephone calls to persons as listed in the parish roster. Include names of bearers in the church bulletin.

Children are expected to accompany their parents. Couples are invited to serve together, even if one is of another faith.

Members of the parish are encouraged to serve as gift bearers on special occasions such as anniversaries, birthdays, or family reunions. If persons serve on such occasions it should be mentioned in the church bulletin.

Assist in Selecting and Training Lectors

1. Set up criteria for selection:

A. Good speaking voice with careful diction

B. Dependable

C. Comfortable before large groups

D. Commanding but warm presence

E. Neat and clean appearance

F. Unflappable (in event of grievous vocal error)

G. Knowledgeable about language, liturgy, and Scripture

2. During training sessions make these suggestions to the lectors:

A. Locate readings according to appropriate cycle.

B. Prepare for readings in advance, and follow procedures carefully.

C. Arrive at church on schedule—never late.

D. Make sure that the lectionary, book of gospels, and petitions are in place, properly marked and tabbed before each Mass.

E. Check in advance that the microphone has been turned on and is placed properly.

F. Ask presider for special instructions before each Mass. This is especially important during RCIA rites, holy days of obligation, Advent, Christmas, Lent, Triduum, Easter.

3. During the training process assist the priest in guiding candidates through each phase of the procedure. Encourage them to practice until they feel comfortable.

4. Set up a schedule for assigning lectors and commentators.

5. Indispensable for lectors is the *Workbook for Lectors and Gospel Readers,* by Aelred Rosser (Liturgy Training Publications). In addition to readings, it offers commentary and marginal notes to help lectors understand the selections they are reading. It points to difficult pronunciations, marks passages for stresses and pauses. Also recommended is the booklet, *The Ministry*

The Lector's Prayer

Father in Heaven,
thank you for a voice that can be heard by those gathered here.
Help me to address these people with humility,
and to deepen their worship experience.
I ask in the name of Jesus, your Son. Amen.

of Lectors by James A. Wallace (Liturgical Press).

Assist in Recruiting and Selecting Cantors

What does a parish look for in a cantor? A pleasing voice, of course. Also a knowledge and appreciation of liturgical music, and skill in leading songs. The congregation appreciates a person with a personality that is relaxed and sincere, dependable and dedicated, one who is neat and clean in appearance.

These qualities should be kept in mind when working with the music director in selecting a cantor.

It is well to choose someone who works easily with the organist and lector. If your parish is located near a college or school of music ask for recommendations from a member of the faculty.

The Cantor's Prayer

Our loving Father,
you have blessed us
with the beauty
of language and music.
I pray that you be with me,
your servant,
as I offer words of prayer,
and songs of praise
in the company of
people gathered here.
I ask this in the name of Jesus,
your Son. Amen.

Train and Supervise Acolytes, Altar Servers, or Altar Attendants

Boys and girls (in nearly every diocese), age ten and older, qualify to participate in altar server ministry. Requirements include a willing spirit, a commitment to serve as needed each month, and attendance at orientation and training sessions. A flyer promoting this ministry is printed on the following page.

1. After servers have been selected, set up a program to train, schedule, and supervise them.

2. Encourage parents to join youngsters at the first training session.

   A. The pastor and the instructor may decide to present opening remarks almost as a pep talk. They should point out that altar servers play an essential role in the ministry. Stress teamwork, dependability, punctuality, proper deportment.

3. At the second training session, outline duties in detail.

   A. Explain where sign-in sheets are kept, give location of albs, candles, tapers, matches, candle extinguisher, the sacramentary, bells, patens.

   B. Explain procedures during the entrance procession, the opening prayer, the liturgy of the Eucharist.

   C. Decide who handles the corporal, the sacramentary, the chalice; who goes forward with the priest to receive the bread and wine; who receives the collection; who takes the water, bowl, and towel to the altar; who rings the bell after the consecration. Describe how these duties are performed.

CATHEDRAL OF THE INCARNATION

Altar Servers Ministry

Cathedral Parishioners—Come one, come all!

Girls and boys, age 10 and over, are invited to participate in the Cathedral Altar Servers Ministry.

Needed:

- Willing spirit
- Commitment to serve 2 Sundays per month
- Attendance at the two orientation and training sessions

ORIENTATION AND TRAINING SESSIONS

Monday, September 19
7:00-8:30 PM
Altar servers and parents

Sunday, September 25
2:00-4:00 PM
Altar servers (parents optional)

If you are interested, please complete the form below and drop it in the collection basket. **DEADLINE TO SIGN-UP IS SUNDAY, SEPT. 11.**

Name: _____ Age: _____

Address: _____

City: _____ State: _____ Zip:_____

Phone: (days) _____ (eve.) _____

Parent's Name: _____

D. Outline duties and procedures during the communion rite and dismissal and, finally, review duties after the Mass.

4. Guide apprentices as they practice, practice, practice.

5. Remind altar servers that duties should be carried out quietly and with dedication. Encourage them to offer a prayer upon arrival, to move without hurrying and, always, to perform duties in a spirit of reverence.

6. Try to develop a camaraderie among altar servers. On a quarterly basis, for example, treat the group to a ball game, with attendant hot dogs and soda pop. Take them bowling, swimming, or to a concert or a movie.

7. An excellent guidebook for altar servers is *Called to Serve*, by Father Albert J. Nevins, published by Our Sunday Visitor, Inc.

The Altar Server's Prayer
Our loving Father,
we thank you for the privilege
of being part of
this ministry of service.
We ask for your
guidance and direction
in this place of worship.
Help us perform our duties
in a manner that will promote
peace, comfort, and consolation.
We pray in the name of Jesus,
your Son. Amen.

Assist in Recruiting and Training Ushers

In recruiting ushers try to approach organizations with likely candidates, such as the Knights of Columbus, the Legion of Mary, the CYO, young married groups, professional groups, senior groups. You need persons who are mature and dedicated, prompt and dependable, neatly dressed, agreeable, and outgoing.

During training make these suggestions:

1. The ministry of the usher is to greet and seat, handle collections, and attend to any problems that may arise.

2. If you find you will be absent, notify the head usher in advance.

3. Arrive early. See that pews are tidy, the gifts table in order, collection baskets ready, and an adequate supply on hand of leaflets to be distributed.

4. Welcome all arrivals. See that each arrival is provided a Sunday bulletin. Give special leaflets to visitors and newcomers.

5. Guide persons to seats in front first. Leave the back of the church for latecomers. Consider roping off a few pews at the rear of the church for latecomers.

6. Seat latecomers at appropriate times (as the congregation is rising or being seated, after the opening prayer, after the Gospel reading, just before the offering—never during the homily or during prayer).

7. If a nursery is available, families with small children should be made aware of it.

8. Adjust blinds or curtains if sun is too bright; adjust temperature if church is too hot or too cold.

9. After the collection, one usher leads the procession, another assists gift bearers.

10. Some churches ask ushers to stand at each row of pews as occupants file up to communion.

Support and Assist Music Directors

A hearty tribute is due those who make music: the music director, the organist, members of the choir. These dedicated and talented people create the proper mood and feeling for every service. They enhance participation and set the pace. They soothe, inspire, and bring richness to the liturgy.

Most music directors are creative people. They vary their programs by offering vocal solos, duets, quartets, sextets, or women's groups for special numbers.

Some organize a men's chorus for Gregorian chants. Some form children's choirs, or even voice-speaking choirs. At times they ask musicians from the congregation to take part in numbers requiring string or wind instruments. They invite outside soloists in for special numbers. They present Christmas, Easter, and other seasonal concerts. They organize vocal groups for special church gatherings.

The ability to read music easily is not always required of choir members. However, for those interested, it might be beneficial to offer 15 to 30 minutes of basic reading before weekly choir rehearsals.

Training should include note recognition, time and measure, the rests, the do, re, mi's and the fa, sol, la's.

In addition to favorite music standbys, thoughtful directors occasionally select difficult or challenging numbers because they know music discovery can be an enriching experi-

ence. For full appreciation, as selections are introduced, directors tell something of the composer or background of the piece.

A good choir is family, and music is a strong bond. There's usually a lot of sharing, caring, and pot luck suppers among choir members (or at least there should be).

Read the booklet, *The Ministry of Musicians* by Edward J. McKenna (Liturgical Press).

Handbell Ringers

Bellringers make beautiful music. To hear a good group is to listen to notes of soaring silver. To hear a mediocre group is merely "wonderful."

Prices for a three-octave set (39 bells) start at $1,500. For a five-octave set (65 bells) expect to pay at least $2,500. Less expensive sets are square-type bells whose prices are in the $700-$800 range.

The Usher's Prayer

Dear Father in heaven,
we thank you for
your precious gift,
the sharing of the Holy Spirit.
Help us to welcome the people
who enter this place of worship.
Guide us in serving them
with love and understanding,
patience and compassion,
serenity and composure.
We ask this in the name of Jesus,
your Son. Amen.

Bells, made of brass or steel, are selected on basis of "temperament." One listens for purity of tone, clarity, and length of ring. Some excellent bell sets come from Schulmerich Carillons and Malmark Bells, both in Pennsylvania.

Two good books to get you started are *Handbell Ringing,* by Robert Ivy, published by Hope, Inc., in Illinois; and *Mastering Musicianship in Handbells,* by Don Allured, published by Broadman Press in Nashville.

Children's Liturgy of the Word

This program tailors the liturgy to children's spiritual needs and gives them a feeling of distinction. Children, ages five to ten, are invited to leave the sanctuary after the opening prayer for a meeting room in the church. There they hear the same readings as the Sunday assembly is using, but the homily covers issues closer to their lives.

The usual agenda is as follows:

1. Children listen to the Scripture reading.

2. They sing the responsorial psalm and gospel acclamation.

3. They hear the Gospel.

4. They listen to the homily.

5. They make a profession of faith, and offer prayers of general intercession.

It should be pointed out that the children's liturgy of the word is not a class or a time to do craft projects. It is a ritual patterned after the liturgy in the Sunday assembly, an interval when children celebrate the God of their own lives.

The children return to the assembly in time to take part in the liturgy of the Eucharist.

To inaugurate such a program, review plans with your pastor and liturgical ministers, and set up a schedule.

Look over materials that are available. Treehaus Communications, Inc., offers the *Sunday Liturgy of the Word and Catechetical Planning Guides* for children ages 6 to 13, which it publishes and mails quarterly. Other Treehaus publications include the *Sunday Lectionary of Readings* and *The Sunday Weekly Leader Guide.*

On page 109 is a sample flyer that can be adapted to promote and interpret the children's liturgy of the word program.

Spiritual Retreats

Consider these steps in conducting a retreat:

1. Site: Look for easy access, adequate parking, quiet environment, climate control, clean rest rooms, adequate large group meeting areas, clean facilities for food preparation, adequate communications. If an overnight retreat, look for suitable sleep accommodations including blankets in the winter, window screens in the summer.

2. Program: Outline and develop the program, recruit suitable speakers as well as song, group, and meditation leaders.

3. Remember to provide handout materials as needed, songbook and devotional materials, pads and pencils, tables, chairs, lecterns, easels, coffee, soft drinks, ice and refreshments, first aid supplies, and emergency aids.

Prayer Programs

One such parish-wide plan is EMMAUS, originated by Mrs. Ann Krenson of the Nashville Diocese. Participants build their faith vision through shared prayer, study, reflection, and action. The program provides opportunity for parishioners to belong to small faith communities of eight to ten people, which link with the

ST. MARY PARISH
MINISTRY TO CHILDREN

At present, St. Mary Parish offers these classes for children:

- Infants to 18 months: Nursery on Sundays during 10:00 o'clock Mass
- 19 months to three years: Toddler Nursery on Sundays during 10 o'clock Mass
- Three to five-year-olds: class on Sundays during 10:00 o'clock Mass
- Kindergarten through sixth grade: class on Sundays 8:45 A.M. to 9:45 A.M.
- 7th grade through high school: class on Sundays 4:45 to 5:45 P.M.

In Advent we will begin celebrating the Liturgy of the Word with Children during the 10:00 o'clock Mass.

After the opening prayer, children ages 6 to 10 years old will be invited to another part of the church to celebrate the liturgy of the word on their level. They will use the same readings as the Sunday assembly, but their homily will apply to the issues of their lives. Children will:

- Hear the first reading,
- Sing the responsorial psalm and gospel acclamation,
- Hear the Gospel,
- Share the homily,
- Make a profession of faith, and
- Offer prayers of general intercession.

Children will then return to the Sunday assembly, where they will rejoin their families for the liturgy of the Eucharist.

Liturgy of the Word with Children is in need of volunteers to:

- Provide leadership with the homily,
- Provide leadership with the music,
- Provide leadership with art and environment,
- Assist the leaders, and
- Assist the children.

**Those interested in helping are invited to an informational meeting at 8 A.M. Sat., November 5, in the education building.
For more information call Melanie Cutler at 555-2996.**

What a great way to make stories of our faith more accessible to our young members. We hope you will be part of this effort!

larger community in shared social action. Small faith communities meet during Lent and Advent.

On page 111 is an announcement and reservation form for a retreat sponsored by the Cathedral of the Incarnation in Nashville, Tennessee. The flyer was distributed by placement in pews and by personal handout at the church door.

Prayer Network

In Chapter 3, page 53, is the outline of a telephone network program. A similar structure is put into action for the parish prayer network.

Those who wish to be added to the prayer list are told to call the network chairperson. In turn, the chairperson calls seven members of the prayer committee to pass along the name of this person, plus the names of other persons who have requested prayers.

Before beginning their prayers, these committee members call seven more persons, which means that fifty persons are praying for the persons in need. Calls are made to the same committee members on the same day each week, so teams are expecting them.

Altar Flowers

Flowers have been called "the unspoken language" of liturgical worship. They can add the finishing touch to a meaningful worship experience while renewing an awareness of beauty and elegance.

"Through the ages the church has used flowers as an important symbol of life, just as it has used candles as symbols of light," according to Wayne Suite, a well-known Tennessee artist and florist.

He thinks many elements should be introduced into altar arrangements in addition to flowers. "In the fall, masses of autumn foliage are impressive. At Thanksgiving, baskets of fresh vegetables or fruit lead to thoughts of gratitude for the munificence of the season. There are times when green plants and potted flowers can be used effectively." He points out that human life began in a garden. The Bible makes reference to gardens 17 times, and to flowers nine times.

1. Encourage parishioners to place flowers on the altar in memory of loved ones.

2. Allow them to arrange their own memorial flowers.

3. Encourage them to grow flowers for church use. With this in mind, cooperate with the parish life committee in offering training in cultivation of altar flowers and church flower arrangement.

Training in Cultivation of Altar Flowers

Gardening is the great American pastime. Surprisingly, however, many would-be gardeners do not understood the science of sun and shade or how deep to plant, how often to water, how much (or little) to fertilize. Many earnest but unschooled weeders seize seedlings along with unwanted plants. Others may view enemy insects as harmless but list among their enemies the bountiful ladybug or pious praying mantis.

Cooperate with the altar society in organizing parish classes in cultivating altar flowers. Suggestions for instructors: a successful gardener, a florist, the manager of a garden store, a nursery operator, a farm agent, a 4-H Club leader, etc.

A wonderful thing about gardening is the time delay from planting to pruning. Results

Cathedral Parish Reflection Day

When: Saturday, May 13, 1995

Where: St. Albert Hall (2nd floor)

What: A time to draw closer to Jesus and listen. This day of silence is offered to you as an opportunity of quiet and peace. You may partake in the day by being present in the morning, afternoon, or all day. Lunches will be provided for those who pre-register. Please feel free to attend if you do not pre-register, but remember to bring your own lunch.)

REFLECTION DAY SCHEDULE:

8:00 AM	Mass in church (optional)
8:30 AM	Coffee/donuts in St. Albert Hall
9:00 AM	Orientation
9:10 AM	First conference: Mary Lou Gorman of St. Thomas Hospital.
10:10 AM	Personal time for private prayer, spiritual reading, reflection
11:30 AM	Lunch in St. Albert Hall (3rd floor)
12:30 PM	Personal time for private prayer, spiritual reading, reflection
1:00 PM	Rosary in chapel (optional)
2:00 PM	Second conference: Diana McQuady
3:00 PM	Closing
3:30 PM	Reconciliation in church (optional)

- Plenty of space for solitude or community prayer
- Bring your walkman to listen to tapes (your own or one from the library)
- the church library will be open
- If you have questions call Esther Cooke (555-2912) or Diana McQuady (555-8643)
- Fill in below & put in collection basket

....

Name: _____

Address: _____

Telephone Number: _____

I plan to attend (please tell us how many people):

All day: _____ Morning only: _____ Afternoon only: _____

I would like the provided lunch: _____

Diet Restrictions: _____

_____

Sample flyer for a parish retreat. See pages 108, 110.

come after months of effort and love and patience. Schedule your class in Spring or early Summer. Present each participant a packet of seed. Coordinate the project by selecting flowers that mature together, and assign each person a specific plant to cultivate.

It is hoped that participants will cultivate flowers especially for the church altar. Class members might harvest their flowers to be used for a special worship service. In addition, their gardening skills could well be used to beautify boxes or borders on the grounds of the church.

Church Flower Arrangement

If there are florists or skilled flower arrangers in your congregation ask them to share their knowledge with fellow parishioners by instructing a class in flower arrangement.

Look for a business firm to underwrite expenses such as costs of florist tape and wire, Styrofoam, Oasis blocks, modeling clay, flowers.

Ask class members to bring their own vases and snips or shears. Select extra-large vases because arrangements should be visible throughout the church.

Include in church bulletin the names of persons responsible for flowers, and names of those being remembered.

Assist in Training the Sacristan

Your church may not have a sacristan as such. In some churches the sacristan's tasks are handled by the altar society, the custodian, various volunteers, or the priest.

Most responsibilities of the sacristan require knowledge, training, and plenty of practice. Here are a few specific duties:

1. Clean, maintain, store, and lay out vestments for priests and altar servers. Be aware of liturgical colors such as:

Green for Ordinary Time.

Red for commemorations of our Lord's passion (including Passion Sunday, Good Friday), Pentecost, feasts of martyrs, apostles, and evangelists.

Violet for Advent and Lent. Some use Rose for Gaudete Sunday (Third Sunday of Advent) and Laetare Sunday (Fourth Sunday of Lent).

White for Christmas and Easter seasons and other occasions of the joyful mysteries. Sometimes used for funerals. (Black and violet are also used for funerals.)

The correct color is listed each day in the church's official Ordo, which should be in every sacristy.

2. Maintain vestments and liturgical linens. Become familiar with the name and use of each

---

A Special Project

Encourage gardeners to cultivate flowers of the Holy Land. Examples include scarlet anemone, garland chrysanthemum, cistus, cornflower, crowfoot, honeysuckle, pink flax, blue lupin, morning glory, white mustard, polyanthus narcissus, pentagonia, poppy, ranunculus, saffron, thicket rose, tulip, and vetchling, along with blossoms of almond, pomegranate, olive, and fig trees.

item, i.e., the alb, amice, cassock, chasuble, cope, dalmatic, stole, and surplice, as well as the benediction veil, the cincture, girdle, maniple, and scapular. Become familiar with such liturgical linens as the altar cloth, chalice veil, corporal, and purificator. See that all are mended, clean, and wrinkle free.

3. Clean, polish, and maintain liturgical items. Learn their proper names and functions:

   A. Sacred objects include altar bells, the aspergillum, brazier, ciborium, incense boat, lavabo dish, incense thurible.

   B. Sacred vessels include the ampulla and cruets, the capsula, the chalice, the ciborium, the lunette, monstrance, paten, and pyx.

   C. Ecclesiastical furniture includes the altar, ambo, podium, credence table, kneelers, and chairs.

   D. Other sacred items include crosses, candlesticks, statues, icons, paintings.

   E. Remember that consecrated oils are kept in a cupboard called the ambry. The Eucharist rests in the ciborium which, in turn, is stored in a box-like container called the tabernacle. Oil and wine are placed on the credence table near the altar. Altar bells, tapers, and candles are stored in the candle room.

4. Store/maintain books (sacramentary, lectionary, book of gospels).

5. Store/maintain ceremonial items: candles, paschal candles, tabernacle lamp, incense.

6. The baptismal font and holy water fonts should be kept clean.

7. Carpets, lighting fixtures, and windows should be kept clean.

8. Attend to placement and maintenance of floral arrangements.

9. Keep inventory of wine, hosts, and liturgical items.

10. Set up for daily Mass and for funerals.

11. Attend to placement and maintenance of the American flag.

In the chancel, place the American flag on a staff on the right of the priest or speaker as he faces the congregation. The papal flag goes on the speaker's left.

Note that the chancel is that part of the church that includes the altar, space for the clergy and, sometimes, the choir. Anywhere else in the sanctuary place the U.S. flag on the right of the congregation as the people face

---

Special Times for Flying the American Flag

New Year's Day, January 1

Presidential Inauguration Day, January 20 (every fourth year)

Lincoln's Birthday, February 12

Washington's Birthday, February 22

Mother's Day, the second Sunday in May

Armed Forces Day, the third Saturday in May

Memorial Day, May 30

Father's Day, the Third Sunday in June

Flag Day, June 14

Independence Day, July 4

Labor Day, the first Monday in September

Constitution and Citizenship Day, September 17

Columbus Day, October 12

Veterans Day, November 11

Thanksgiving Day, the fourth Thursday in November

front. The papal flag goes on the congregation's left.

The national flag should never be used as a decoration. Instead use red/white/blue bunting, arranged with blue at top.

Sacristans should have an understanding of celebrations and sacraments. A helpful reference is *The Order of Prayer in the Liturgy of the Hours and Celebration of the Eucharist, The Ordo* (Paulist Press).

Another very helpful resource for sacristans is *The Sacristy Manual*, by G. Thomas Ryan (Liturgy Training Publications).

The Sacristan's Prayer

Lord, and Loving Father,
Guide my hands as I serve in your house this day.
Guide my heart as I seek to prepare a place for your glory and veneration.
I pray that all who worship here will grow in love and service to you.
I ask this in the name of Jesus. Amen.

Chapter 9

Missions

A missions team or committee helps to coordinate and to conduct the outreach of the parish. When recruiting members for this committee, look for parishioners who can give strong spiritual support to the church's outreach program: people of various backgrounds (racial, ethnic, economic, etc.), business persons, economists, physicians, nurses, persons devoted to the propagation of the Christian faith, deacons, members of such organizations as the Legion of Mary, Knights of Columbus, and Cursillo.

Goal
• To promote knowledge of, devotion to, and support of missions.

Objectives
1. Adopt a parish outside the U.S.
2. Assist a poor parish in the inner city.
3. Support a home mission area.
4. Sponsor a lay missionary nurse, teacher, or other person to assist adopted mission.
5. Sponsor programs to generate prayer and financial assistance to missions and spiritual outreach.
6. Promote Mission Week in October.
7. Promote and support such missionary presences as the Claretians, the Columban Fathers, the Comboni Missionaries, Glenmary Home Missioners, Maryknoll Fathers, Missionhurst, the Salesians, the Missionaries of St. Charles (serving migrant and refugee people), the Christian Appalachian Project (serving depressed areas of Appalachia).
8. See that the inventory of your parish library includes adequate literature on home and foreign Missions.

SPECIFIC PROJECTS IN DETAIL

Adopt a Mission Outside the U.S.
1. The Adopt-A-Parish program offers an opportunity to assist impoverished churches in Third World countries in ever-widening areas. It allows parishes, prayer groups, individuals, and organizations to send funds directly to an adopted parish, school, or religious community. At this writing the program has extended into Jamaica, the Dominican Republic, Mexico, India, and the Central American countries of El Salvador, Guatemala, Nicaragua, and Panama.

Essentially Pope John Paul II envisioned a program such as Adopt-A-Parish when he pleaded for more catechists to teach the world's three billion unbaptized.

The program was begun in 1978 by a Canadian-born, Catholic layman named Harry Hosey. In an age of bureaucratic red tape, this man and his wife put together a simple, effective operation with no middlemen and no administrative charges.

"Every cent of money entrusted to us," they emphasize, "goes directly to those in need of it."

For full information, write Harry Hosey, Director, Adopt-A-Parish Program, P.O. Box 111, Old Hickory, TN 37138; 615-847-5022.

2. A similar agency is the Haiti Parish Twinning Program, a nonprofit organization that originated through efforts of Mr. Hosey and Theresa Patterson. For full information write Ms. Patterson, Director, Haiti Parish Twinning Program, 208 Leake Avenue, Nashville, TN 37205; 615-356-4454.

The Mission Statement of the Haiti Twinning Program:

A. To encourage linkages between Catholic parishes and institutions in Haiti and parishes, institutions, and individuals in the United States and Canada,

B. To develop models for parish actions,

C. To encourage prayerful solidarity with our sisters and brothers in Haiti,

D. To provide resources and support in religious, educational, medical, and economic areas, and

E. To promote an awareness among Catholics of the injustices present in Haiti and our gospel call to respond.

With the assistance of American and Canadian parishes, pastors in Haiti can help the people help themselves. Money is used to build hospitals, dispensaries, and nutrition centers, fund nursing and medical assistance, pay teachers, and help catechists.

Twinning or linking with a parish in Haiti is a simple process, Ms. Patterson points out. Arrangements can be made for a representative from the Twinning Program to provide color slides and information to a parish or parish council. Once the decision to twin is made, pictures and information are provided on a specific Haitian parish.

It is recommended that a Haiti committee be

Assist a Poor Parish in the Inner City Area

In cooperation with the diocese select an inner city parish with problems that can be addressed by your parish.

1. List specific problems or needs of the inner city parish.

2. Outline a plan to address each problem. Plan actions to be taken by the inner city parish with assistance of members of your parish.

3. Set deadlines.

4. Recruit volunteer workers.

5. Seek resources to lend assistance (Boy/Girl Scouts, YMCA/YWCA, mental health groups, drug council centers, Habitat for Humanity, Salvation Army, American Red Cross, businesses, foundations, grants).

6. Put plan into action.

established. Such a committee is responsible for maintaining awareness and for keeping communication flowing between the Haitian pastor and the U.S. congregation. The Haiti Parish Twinning Program publishes the *Haitian Connection* every two months, which is a source for sharing ideas, projects, fund-raising, and experiences of those who have visited Haiti.

The Haitian pastor provides reports on life, activities, and projects in his parish, and tells how funds have been used.

To fund the Twinning Program most sponsoring parishes have second collections, but some tithe or give a percentage of their weekly collection. Often special fund-raising events are organized. Sponsors are assured that one hundred percent of every donation goes directly to the Haitian project.

Today the Haiti program includes more than 250 twinnings, making it the largest citizen-to-citizen network linking the United States and Haiti.

The U.S. parish that twins a parish in Haiti or adopts a parish in another part of the world should expect to send representatives each year to visit the sister parish. There, the visiting delegation will offer encouragement and guidance, review accomplishments and problems, and determine primary needs for the upcoming year. In addition they should take photographs for sharing, and perhaps procure craft items to be sold in fund-raising efforts.

Upon returning, the delegation should make a full report to the church membership. It is well to reinforce verbal reports with printed material, prepare a display for the bulletin board, and write an article for the church newsletter.

Prayer and Financial Assistance

Give a dollar to a missionary and watch it grow.

In impoverished countries local products usually are inexpensive, as is labor, so contributions go far.

There's a place for every donation of whatever size. As Claretian missionaries point out, "Small contributions help provide Bibles, missals, and educational material…larger contributions may be spent for power generators…or to build and repair chapels and mission buildings."

How does a parish raise money for missions? Let me count the ways:

1. Your diocese can obtain kits containing posters, bulletin announcements, cardboard rice bowls, and other material from Catholic Relief Services (209 W. Fayette, Baltimore, Maryland 21201; 301-625-2220). Parishioners are asked to deprive themselves during Lent and put money saved into the rice bowl for Catholic relief.

2. Ask members of your parish to set aside their own wide-mouth bottles, drawstring bags, or piggy banks for mission savings.

 A. Deposit a fixed amount each day for a specified period. For example, make a donation each day in Lent, each day in Advent, each day of the work week, each day your favorite sports team plays a game, or each Sunday in daylight savings time (from April when clocks spring forward to October when they fall back).

 B. Take the plan seriously. Make deposits regularly. Send your check with a prayer to the mission field.

3. As an incentive to the weight conscious (up or down), make a private pledge to place $10 in the missions plate for every pound lost or gained.

4. Pancakes for 50, anyone? On the first or

fourth Sunday of the month, schedule a pancake breakfast. Serve with bacon and coffee at a price that will allow you to add to the mission barrel. The secret of good coffee is given in Chapter 6. Below is a recipe that is guaranteed to make pancake history.

---

100 BUTTERMILK PANCAKES

Dry ingredients. Combine in large bowl:

4½ pounds All Purpose Flour
12 ounces Granulated Sugar
4 ounces Baking Powder
1 tablespoon Salt

Wet ingredients. Mix in a separate bowl:

12 Eggs
3½ quarts Buttermilk
12 ounces Vegetable Oil
1 tablespoon Baking Soda

Mix. Beat until frothy, add to dry ingredients. Stir until mixed. Spoon onto griddle preheated to 350 degrees Fahrenheit. Turn when bubbles appear and cake is golden brown. Each 4-inch pancake contains less than 150 calories. For more calories serve with maple syrup.

(This recipe comes from Food for Fifty, *by Grace Shugart and Mary Molt, published by Macmillan Publishing Company. It is used with permission.)*

---

5. When eating out, match the server's tip with an equal amount for missions. Fast one day a week and donate money saved. Or, at the end of the day, empty your pocket change into a canister for missions.

6. Collect aluminum cans. When you have a sizeable number pay a visit to the recycling center. Rates are based on quantity and run from 38 to 50 cents a pound in most areas. Approximately 30 cans make a pound.

7. Conduct a paper drive. Prices on collected paper vary according to demand. Of interest to ecologists: If you subscribe to a morning and evening city newspaper (5 sections each) you will accumulate about 2,000 pounds of paper a year. That's a ton. Although paper mills grow their own trees, they fell 17 of them for each ton of paper produced.

8. Schedule a biannual sale of craft products from your mission field. Artists in your adopted parish can thus find a market for their products, and your parishioners will be made aware of families receiving their support.

9. A number of retail outlets, especially chain

stores, offer reimbursement for cash register receipts—some refunds total much as five percent. Check with stores in your community.

Ask parishioners to place receipts in collection baskets along with their gifts each Sunday. Churches can realize significant amounts of money for missions through such collections.

10. Sponsor a food co-operative program through which parishioners can order bulk food at discount prices. The church receives a percentage of the profits.

A number of companies offer such programs, including the Market Day Corporation, headquartered in Chicago. It publishes monthly price lists and order forms that parishioners are asked to complete and return. Products are delivered to a specified location for pickup.

11. There's always Bingo! In some states this grand old church money maker is against the law. If so, you will have to be creative in other areas.

12. Conduct a clothing drive, but first—and this is important—make sure you will be able to deliver the clothing to its destination *and* that the people are definitely in need of it.

If you do decide to collect clothing see that all items are clean, mended, sorted, and sized. When you make your appeal remind donors that items should be appropriate: Eskimos seldom wear beach sandals, for example, and Haitians have no need for gloves or overcoats.

Promote Mission Week

1. Cooperate with the communications committee in planning and implementing plans to promote Mission Week and Mission Sunday in October.

2. Begin in early September so plans can be completed and programs in place by October 1.

3. Prepare a special liturgy for Mission Week.

4. Sponsor a forum on spiritual outreach with an active or retired missionary as speaker.

5. Prepare a special bulletin board display.

6. Stock your literature rack with special mission material.

Literature on Missions

Your library subscription list should include such magazines and newsletters as:

Missionhurst (4651 N. 25th St., Arlington, VA 22207; 703-528-3804)

Maryknoll (missionary work overseas; Maryknoll, NY 10545; 914-941-7590)

Mountain Spirit (Christian Appalachian Project, 322 Crab Orchard Road, Lancaster, KY 40446; 606-792-3051)

The Glenmary Challenge (home missions; PO Box 465618, Cincinnati, OH 45246-5618; 513-874-8900)

Mission (Society for the Propagation of the Faith, 366 Fifth Avenue, New York, NY 10001; 212-563-8700)

Mission Handbook (U.S. Catholic Mission Association, 3029 Fourth St., NE, Washington, DC 20017; 202-832-3112)

Extension (home missions; 35 E. Wacker Drive-Suite 400, Chicago, IL 60601-2105; 312-236-7240)

Missionaries of Africa Report (1624 21st St., NW, Washington, DC 20009; 202-232-5154)

The Mission Messenger (Indian missions; PO Box 610, Thoreau, NM 87323; 505-862-7847)

Mission Update (global missions; 3029 Fourth St., NE, Washington, DC 20017; 202-832-3112)

Appendix

Time and Talent Survey, Pages 123-124

Every parish faces special problems. Most find it difficult to find volunteer workers. Others sorely need a church census but aren't sure of the procedure.

The Time and Talent survey shown on pages 123-124 is designed as an appeal for volunteers, but the first section will serve as an excellent census form. An added feature is that it can be adapted for card file or computer use.

For effective use as a recruitment aid, the sheet should be accompanied by explanations of the positions listed. Luckily, most assignments remain the same so, once completed, parishes can use the same form year after year.

Sample Greeting Cards for the Parish, Pages 125-129

Beginning on page 125 are some samples of computer-generated greeting and "touch" cards. Often the very best cards are the ones designed for your own parishioners. Formats for greeting cards are available through a number of software programs, including Print Shop by Bröderbund and Cardshop Plus.

Suggested formats given here are for New Baby, Birthday, Get Well, Anniversary, and Sympathy cards. Pages are designed to be made from an 8½ X 11" sheet of paper, folded to a 5½ X 4¼" which will fit a standard 4⅜ X 5¾" envelope. Gray fold lines are shown on the sample to help you place the type and illustrations in their proper positions.

ALL SAINTS CHURCH

706 Mary Street, Farley, Illinois 60201
Telephone 708-555-6020

Census Information

All members of All Saints Parish are asked to complete this census form. Optional information is requested to keep the church office informed of your skills, talents, and interests.

❏ Mr. & Mrs.   ❏ Mr.   ❏ Mrs.   ❏ Miss   ❏ Ms.

NAME: _____

ADDRESS: _____(City)_____ (ZIP)_____

TELEPHONE: (Home) _____ (Work) _____

Number of children under 15 years of age: _____ Names: _____

Optional Information

Read the lists below. Check boxes for areas in which you have an interest or in which you would be willing to serve

I. Parish Pastoral Council
100 ❏ Will serve on Council

101 ❏ Will serve on committee

II. Administration and Stewardship
200 ❏ Will serve as needed
201 ❏ Bookkeeper
202 ❏ Computer Operator
203 ❏ Fund Raiser
204 ❏ Financial Specialist
205 ❏ Inventory Coordinator
206 ❏ Personnel Specialist
207 ❏ Carpenter/Woodworker

208 ❏ Electrician
209 ❏ Gardener/Grounds Keeper
210 ❏ Painter
211 ❏ Plumber
212 ❏ Security Guard
213 ❏ Police Officer
214 ❏ Change outdoor bulletin bd
215 ❏ Misc Buildings/Grounds

III. Communications
300 ❏ Will Serve as Needed
301 ❏ Will Visit Newcomers
302 ❏ Keep Scrapbook
303 ❏ Write Outdoor Bul. Copy
304 ❏ Will Do Indoor Bul. Boards.
305 ❏ Will Do Monthly Calendar
306 ❏ Prepare Parish Directory

307 ❏ Prepare Org/Com Directory
308 ❏ Newsletter Editor
309 ❏ Newsletter Writer
310 ❏ Mail Expediter
311 ❏ Radio /TV Specialist
312 ❏ Coor. Telephone Network
313 ❏ Photographer/Artist

IV. Education and Formation

400 ❏ Serve as Needed
401 ❏ Teach Church School
402 ❏ Assist in Church School
403 ❏ Will be an RCIA Sponsor
404 ❏ Help with RCIA Pgm

405 ❏ Help in Church Nursery
406 ❏ Promote Church Nursery
407 ❏ Will Serve as Librarian
408 ❏ Help Promote Library
409 ❏ Coord classes/training

V. Family Life

500 ❏ Serve as Needed
501 ❏ RNs/LPNs ck bl pressure
502 ❏ Assist in Health Fairs
503 ❏ Coord Seasonal Programs
504 ❏ Coord Singles Programs
505 ❏ Coord Marriage Prep Pgm

506 ❏ Coordinate Young Adult Pgms
507 ❏ Coord Pgms for Elderly
508 ❏ Coord Substance Abuse Pgms
509 ❏ Coord Respect Life Pgms
510 ❏ Coord Pgms for Div/Sep Cath
511 ❏ Coord Pgms for Spec Needs

VI. Parish Life

600 ❏ Serve as Needed
601 ❏ Help with Coffees
602 ❏ Help with Family Nights
603 ❏ Help with Excursions
604 ❏ Help with Open House
605 ❏ Help with Picnic
606 ❏ Will Sew/Crochet
607 ❏ Will Cook

608 ❏ Coord Talent/Skills file
609 ❏ Coord Transportation Pgm
610 ❏ Help with Visitation Pgm
611 ❏ Help with Newcomer Pgm
612 ❏ Help with CYO Pgms
613 ❏ Help with Men's Clubs
614 ❏ Help with Women's Clubs
615 ❏ Will Help with Clean-Up

VII. Social Action

700 ❏ Serve as Needed
701 ❏ Help with Blood Drives
702 ❏ Adult Literacy

703 ❏ Habitat for Humanity
704 ❏ Sponsor Scout Troop
705 ❏ Help in Shelter Program

VIII. Worship and Spiritual Life

800 ❏ Serve as Needed
801 ❏ Serve as Lector
802 ❏ Serve as Cantor
803 ❏ Serve as Altar Server
804 ❏ Serve as Usher

805 ❏ Serve as Sacristan
806 ❏ Help with Prayer Network
807 ❏ Help with Altar Flower Pgm
808 ❏ Adult/Youth/Children Choir
809 ❏ Handbell Choir

IX. Mission of Spiritual Support

900 ❏ Serve as Needed
901 ❏ Adopt/Parish Program
902 ❏ Haiti Twinning Program

903 ❏ Coord Mission Sunday/Week
904 ❏ Coord Inner City Program
905 ❏ Coord Mission Fund Raising

(Optional): Your Birth Date: _____   Wedding Anniversary: _____

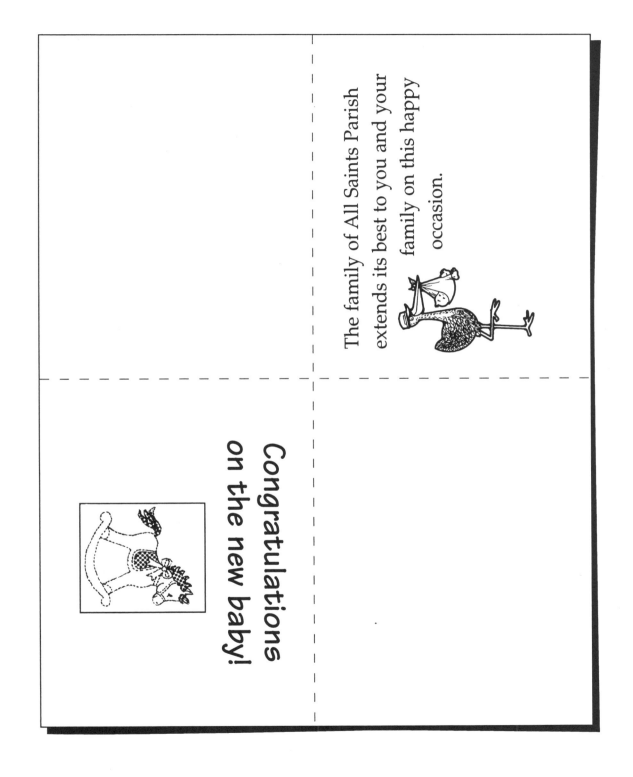

The family of All Saints Parish extends its best to you and your family on this happy occasion.

Congratulations on the new baby!

The parish family
of All Saints
extends best
wishes to you
on your birthday.

Happy
Birthday!

Thinking
of You

Your friends at
All Saints Parish
wish you a quick and
complete recovery.

Happy Anniversary

The All Saints Family joins in wishing you the very best on your anniversary.

With heartfelt sympathy

The families and staff
of All Saints Parish
extend sincere sympathy
to you for your loss.

For Further Reading

Advisory Council Plan: Constitution, By-Laws and Agenda. Advisory Council Plan: Commentary, by James F. Walsh, Jr., Memphis, TN. © 1967.

All-In-One Media Directory. New Paltz, NY: Gebbie Press, Inc. (Annual)

Bulletin Board Ideas, by Bonnie Morris. Nashville, TN: Abingdon Press.

Bulletin Boards and Displays, by Gayle Skaggs. Jefferson, NC: McFarland, 1993.

Called to Serve, A Guidebook for Altar Servers, by Rev. Albert J. Nevins. Huntington, IN: Our Sunday Visitor Publishing Division, 1993.

Capital Campaign Handbook, The, by David J. Hauman. Detroit, MI: Taft Group.

Catechism of the Catholic Church, Liguori, MO: Liguori Publications, 1994.

Catholic Encyclopedia, edited by Rev. Peter M. J. Stravinskas. Huntington, IN: Our Sunday Visitor Publishing Division, Our Sunday Visitor, Inc., 1991.

Catholic Press Directory, Rockville Centre, NY: The Catholic Press Association. (Annual)

The Catholic Source Book, edited by Rev. Peter Klein. Dubuque, IA: Brown Publishing - ROA Media, 1990.

Christian Communicator's Handbook: A Practical Guide to Church Public Relations, by Floyd A. Craig. Nashville, TN: Broadman Press, 1977.

Code of Canon Law, Washington, D.C.: Canon Law Society of America, 1983.

Cooking for Fifty, by Chet Holden. New York, NY: John Wiley & Sons, 1993.

Creating an Effective Parish Pastoral Council, by Robert G. Howes. Collegeville, MN: The Liturgical Press, 1991.

"English as a Second Language," Menlo Park, CA: Addison Wesley, 1992.

Federal Register Part II, Architectural and Transportation Barriers Compliance Board 36 CFR Part 1191. American with Disabilities Act Accessibility Guidelines for Buildings and Facilities, Department of Justice, June 24, 1994.

Federal Register Part III, Architectural and Transportation Barriers Compliance Board 28 CFR Part 36, Nondiscrimination on the Basis of Disability by Public Accommodations and in Commercial Facilities, Department of Justice, July 26, 1991.

Food for Fifty, by Grace Shugart and Mary Molt. New York, NY: Macmillan Publishing Company, 1992.

14,000 Quips and Quotes, by E. C. McKenzie. Grand Rapids, MI: Baker Book House, 1988.

Fund Raising for Non Profit Groups, by Peter Edles. New York: McGraw-Hill, 1988.

Fund Raising Guide to Religious Philanthropy, by Bernard Jankowski. Detroit, MI: Taft Group, 1997.

Guidelines for Parish Councils, by James F. Walsh, Jr., Office of Lay Affairs, Diocese of Nashville, 1972.

Handbell Ringing, by Robert Ivy. Carol Stream, IL: Hope Publishing Company, 1995.

Handbook, Parish Pastoral Councils, Nashville, TN: Diocese of Nashville, Ministry Formation Services, 1989.

The How-to-Do-It Manual for the Amateur Float Builder. Minneapolis, MN: Vaughn Display, 1987.

Keeping Your Parish Financially Healthy, by Harold B. Averkamp. Mahwah, NJ: Paulist Press, 1989.

Literacy and Life Skills. Boston, MA: Heinle Publishers, 1992.

Manual for Financial Development: Fund Raising Made Easy, Volumes I and II, produced by the Public Support Department, American Red Cross. Washington, D.C.: American National Red Cross, 1991.

Mastering Musicianship in Handbells, by Don Allured. Nashville, TN: Broadman Press, 1995.

The Ministry of Communion, by Michael Kwatera, O.S.B.. Collegeville, MN: The Liturgical Press, 1983.

The Ministry of Lectors, by James A. Wallace, C.SS.R. Collegeville, MN: The Liturgical Press, 1981.

The Ministry of Musicians, by Edward J. McKenna. Collegeville, MN: The Liturgical Press, 1983.

The Ministry of the Sacristan, by Frank Winkels. Collegeville, MN: The Liturgical Press, 1989.

The Ministry of Ushers, by Gregory F. Smith. Collegeville, MN: The Liturgical Press, 1980.

Ministry to the Imprisoned, by Joan Campbell, S.P. Collegeville, MN: The Liturgical Press, 1989.

The New Practical Guide for Parish Councils, by William J. Rademacher. Mystic, CT: Twenty-Third Publications, 1988.

The Official Catholic Directory. New Providence, NJ: P. J. Kenedy & Sons, in association with R. R. Bowker, A Reed Reference Publishing Company.

The Order of Prayer in the Liturgy of the Hours and Celebration of the Eucharist or *The Ordo,* Mahwah, NJ: Paulist Press.

Parade and Float Guide, by Leroy Vaughn. Minneapolis, MN: T. S. Denison, 1956.

The Parish Council Handbook, by Robert C. Broderick. Chicago, IL: Franciscan Herald Press, 1968, 1985.

Parish Councils. Renewing the Christian Community, by Bernard Lyons. Techny, IL: Divine Word Publications, 1967.

The Pocket Catholic Dictionary, by John A. Hardon, S. J. New York, NY: Image Books, Doubleday, 1985.

The Raising of Money, by James Gregory Lord. Cleveland, OH: Third Sector Press, 1996.

The RCIA: Transforming the Church, by Thomas H. Morris, Mahwah, NJ: The Paulist Press, 1989.

Recommendations for Accessibility Guidelines: Recreational Facilities and Outdoor Developed Areas, U.S. Architectural and Transportation Barriers Compliance Board, July, 1994.

The Sacristy Manual, by G. Thomas Ryan. Chicago, IL: Liturgy Training Publications, 1995.

The Sharing Community. Parish Councils and their Meaning, by David P. O'Neill. Dayton, OH: Pflaum Press, 1968.

Speaker's Quote Book, by Benjamin R. DeJong. Grand Rapids, MI: Baker Book House, 1994.

The Standard Code of Parliamentary Procedure, by Alice Sturgis, Revised by the American Institute of Parliamentarians. New York, NY: McGraw-Hill, 1993.

Stewardship of Time and Talent. South Deerfield, MA: Channing L. Pete Co., 1974.

"The Sunday Liturgy of the Word and Catechetical Planning Guide." Loveland, OH: Treehaus Communications, Inc.

The Total Parish Manual, by William J. Bausch. Mystic CT: Twenty-Third Publications, 1994.

Training the Parish Lector, by James A. Wallace, C.SS.R. Collegeville, MN: The Liturgical Press. (Videocassette)

Workbook for Lectors and Gospel Readers, by Aelred Rosser. Chicago, IL: Liturgy Training Publications (Annual).

Index

Of Related Interest ...

Called to Parish Ministry
Identity, Challenges and Spirituality of Lay Ministers
Greg Dues and Barbara Walkley

Offers lay ministers guidance, encouragement and support for fulfilling their calling based on the history of the evolving roles of involved lay people in the church.
0-89622-649-2, 176 pp, $12.95 (order M-39)

The Total Parish Manual
Everything You Need to Empower Your Faith Community
William J. Bausch

This is the complete "how-to" for guiding a parish to fulfilling its mission to its members. Covered are topics such as the sacraments, the liturgical year, volunteers, organizations, ministries, small faith communities, evangelization.
0-89622-607-7, 320 pp, $29.95 (order M-03)

The Hands-On Parish
Reflections and Suggestions for Fostering Community
William J. Bausch

Father Bausch shares more than 100 tried and workable ideas for adaptation by other parishes.
0-89622-401-5, 228 pp, $9.95 (order C-08)

New Practical Guide for Parish Councils
William Rademacher and Marliss Rogers

A valuable and important book both for councils that are functioning well and for those struggling to create a viable identity in their faith communities.
0-89622-371-x, 272 pp, $9.95 (order W-81)

Creative Christian Leadership
Skills for More Effective Ministry
Kevin Treston

Helps Christian leaders improve managerial ability, develop their sense of purpose and reach personal and group goals more effectively.
0-89622-648-4, 120 pp, $12.95 (order M-24)

Available at religious bookstores or from:

XXIII TWENTY-THIRD PUBLICATIONS
P.O. Box 180 • Mystic, CT 06355 • 1-800-321-0411